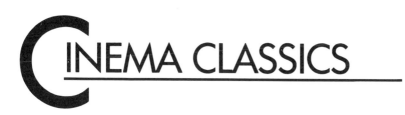

CINEMA CLASSICS

A facsimile reprint series of significant books
on film history, and film criticism, including
a number of important screenplays

Selected by
The American Film Institute
Louis B. Mayer Library

A Garland Series

Hollywood Cameramen

Sources of Light

Charles Higham

Garland Publishing, Inc.
New York & London   1986

For a complete list of the titles in this series
see the final pages of this volume.

This facsimile has been made from a copy in
the Yale University Library.

Reprinted by permission of Martin Secker & Warburg, Limited.
Copyright © 1970 by Charles Higham.

Library of Congress Cataloging-in-Publication Data

Higham, Charles.
  Hollywood cameramen.

  (Cinema classics)
  Reprint. Originally published: Bloomington :
Indiana University Press, 1970.
  Includes index.
  1. Cinematographers—California—Hollywood (Los
Angeles)—Biography. I. Title. II. Series.
TR849.A1H53 1986   778.5'3'0922 [B]   82-49226
ISBN 0-8240-5764-3 (alk. paper)

Design by Donna Montalbano

The volumes in this series are printed on
acid-free, 250-year-life paper.

Printed in the United States of America

Cinema One

14 Hollywood Cameramen

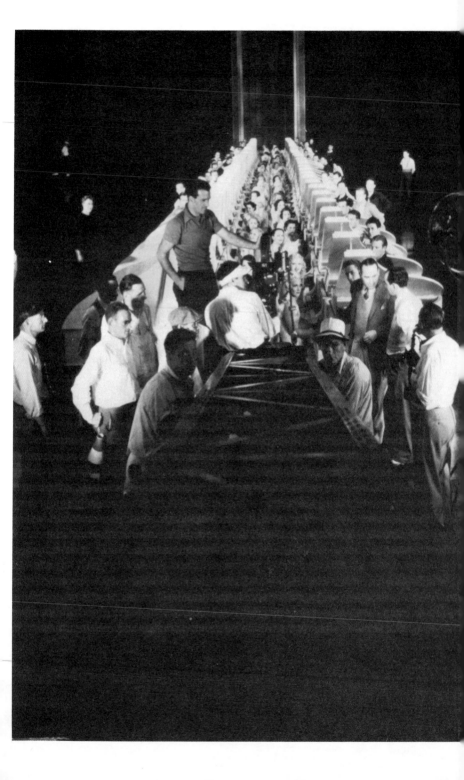

Hollywood Cameramen:
Sources of Light

Charles Higham

Indiana University Press
Bloomington and London

The Cinema One series is published by
Indiana University Press
in association with *Sight and Sound*
and the Education Department of the
British Film Institute

First United States publication 1970

Library of Congress catalog card number: LC 74-115457
ISBN 0 253 13820 5 clothbound
ISBN 0 253 13821 3 paperbound

Printed in Great Britain

Contents

Cover: James Wong Howe and Samantha Eggar on *The Molly Maguires*

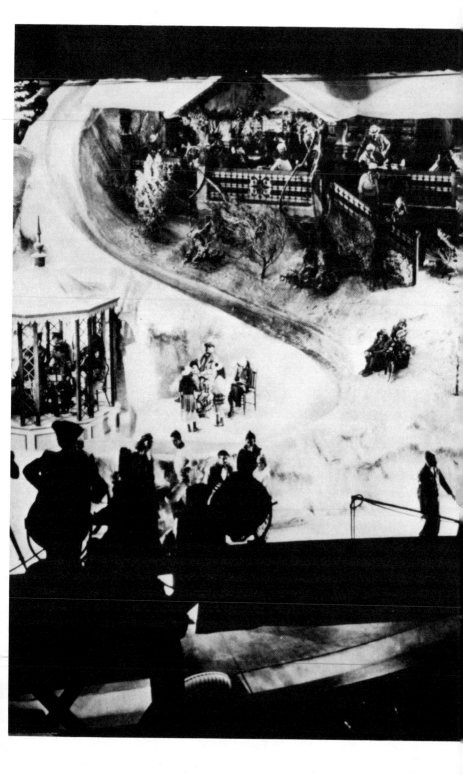

Introduction

A shimmering sky, with a lonely rider at the edge of a canyon, the trees casting hard, razor-edged shadows and, far away in the scrub to the north-west, an Indian fire sending up a snake of smoke. . . . The central image of the American cinema, symbolic and unchanging across seventy years, is still the Western image; and the great cameramen – Lee Garmes, James Wong Howe, William Daniels among them – have created, with the aid of filters and arcs and special lenses, its classic beauty.

With their lighting, either realistic, like Wong Howe's, or painterly, like Lee Garmes's, or symphonic in its range, like Stanley Cortez's, the cameramen have created an American cinema as often bathed in their own vision as in that of a director. Directors, until recent years at least, have been content to establish their signature through the handling of the players, the expert, highly individual handling of dialogue scenes, and the juxtaposition of sequences in the cutting-room. They have left the physical look of a film – often, in fact, its whole physical direction in the matter of the visuals – to specific cinematographers. Only Hitchcock, using light for specific psychological purposes, Welles, creating his own bizarre and baroque world of the imagination through low-key images, Rex Ingram, Clarence Brown, Frankenheimer and Mamoulian among the major figures have fully mastered the secrets of film light.

Of the others, Capra has achieved his effects mainly through a

7

Stage revue set for Rowland V. Lee's *I Am Suzanne* (1933): cameraman, Lee Garmes brilliantly fluid editing style, a command of masses of people, and a constantly moving camera, often in the agile charge of Joseph Walker; but his films are almost never creatively exciting from the lighting point of view. Cukor has been content to express general desires in the matter of lighting, but has little interest in the mechanics; his films vary drastically in their visual texture, their style reposing mainly in the theatrically accomplished handling of the actors. The pyrotechnics of *Gaslight* or *A Woman's Face* or *A Star Is Born* are due entirely to the cameramen concerned, as Cukor himself has admitted.

John Ford is a director of a marked personal style, but again his films look entirely different one from another, the style emerging rather in the personal response to people: affectionate, warm, with a rural decency and intimacy. An Arthur Miller Ford (*How Green Was My Valley, Tobacco Road*), will look, with its shiny surface and brilliant contrasts, entirely different from a Joe August Ford, shadowy and soft, a Bert Glennon Ford, romantically diffused and quietly glowing, an Archie Stout Ford, rough and harsh, with a jolting unevenness of visual tone, or a Gregg Toland Ford, with deep focus and ceilinged sets ahead of *Citizen Kane* (*The Long Voyage Home*).

Billy Wilder's films, too, vary enormously in their images. At his best, as in his films photographed by John F. Seitz, his work has a powerfully grim and grey appearance, stripped of gloss; yet when he uses a less individual cameraman (as in *Meet Whiplash Willie* and *Kiss Me, Stupid*) he is given remarkably flat and washed-out visuals. A director who hates to see lushness on the screen, he is capable of producing indifferent lighting results (as in *Witness for the Prosecution,* one of the most toneless features on record) when his cameraman is not sufficiently strong to impose on the images a visual equivalent for his black vision.

Fritz Lang's *œuvre* suffers from the same unevenness of visual texture: without a Fritz Arno Wagner, an Arthur Miller (*Man Hunt*) or a James Wong Howe (*Hangmen Also Die*) he is apt to fall into the flat monotonies of a *While the City Sleeps* or *Beyond a Reasonable Doubt.* John Frankenheimer's films have had the benefit of a consistently skilled cameraman, Lionel Lindon; but Frankenheimer's art has never looked more exciting than in *Seconds*, which allied him on one single occasion with James Wong Howe.

Even Hitchcock has suffered from the loss of a cameraman capable of bringing his visual ideas to life. When Robert Burks died tragically in a fire, Hitchcock was forced to turn to another cameraman (in *Torn Curtain*), one who provided him with less interesting results. Cameramen, too, have succeeded in varying even this most visually orientated of directors' personal approach: a George Barnes Hitchcock, shadowy and shallow-focused (*Rebecca*), is entirely different from a Lee Garmes Hitchcock, heavily Gothic and touched with a bleak north light (*The Paradine Case*). And the rough, haphazard style of a Charles Lawton, jun. (*The Lady from Shanghai*) could drastically affect the vision of an Orson Welles, more formally expressed in the cold sharpness, the depth of field of a Gregg Toland or the romantic, plushly upholstered style of a Stanley Cortez.

In the work of even the most powerful and individual directors, the lighting cameraman can still find his place; we see his signature on the portrait as well as the director's. And it was in portraiture that so many of the great cameramen began: Charles Rosher, whose talent was to flower unforgettably in *Sunrise*, was a portrait photographer at the dawn of movies, and so was his associate master on that film, Karl Struss; while Stanley Cortez, James Wong Howe and many others began by giving the stars in stills and on the screen the romantic elegance of figures in Victorian miniatures.

When films began to mature in the teens of the century, cameraman and director had distinctly separate functions: the cameraman's job was to make the stars look beautiful and to handle the technically tricky orthochromatic film to give a proper texture to rooms, trees and skies; the director's job was to control the actors, to give the film its momentum through editing and action. It was many years before a cameraman could impart to a film a distinctly personal look, because fashions in photography were endemic and all pervading: female stars had to be backlit with Victorian aureoles like haloes, their faces large, oval, and shimmering; landscapes, filtered through gauze, were given a Pre-Raphaelite glow that again harked back half a century; love scenes were romantically brought to life in images as diffused as those of a saintly *fin de siècle* calendar.

Many directors broke free of these romantic styles: William S. Hart's Westerns had a stark realism, von Stroheim's films also, and Griffith, though overly addicted to gauzes, often achieved a documentary vividness in his location shots. But even Billy Bitzer, Griffith's loyal cameraman, failed to impose any really marked signature of his own above or below his master's, and his addiction to gauze shots was simply conventional, rather than, as so often erroneously reported, original. We deeply admire today the work of William Daniels on the Garbo silents, most notably in the ravishing *Flesh and the Devil*, but he was working in an overall Hollywood tradition in his use of gauzes and filters; and the landscapes of America looked strikingly similar in the work of director after director. The time when that great wilderness could be transformed by a photographer as by a painter had not yet arrived.

It was in the mid twenties, at about the time of the development of panchromatic film in 1924, that strongly individual styles began to emerge. John F. Seitz began to use Rembrandt's north light in films made with Rex Ingram, and the results were markedly individual. Victor Milner and Lee Garmes took up the mode, and transformed it into separate and personal styles. In Garmes's lovely *The Garden of Allah*, directed by Ingram, the north light bloomed superbly, isolating hands and portions of faces, casting deep shadows, making the whole film richly alive. Soon afterwards, Garmes revolutionized the industry, brilliantly developing his own approach by using bare Mazda bulbs to light the whole set in his historic *The Little Shepherd of Kingdom Come*, directed by Alfred Santell.

Meanwhile, James Wong Howe had already begun to establish a signature in the magical effects of Herbert Brenon's films, most notably *Peter Pan*, Arthur Miller's rich images for *Forever* (*Peter Ibbetson*) were, witnesses attest, precursors of his golden age in the forties, and Karl Struss was achieving the miraculous transitions of *Ben Hur*, the lepers cured (without cuts or dissolves) in a filter technique later used in *Dr Jekyll and Mr Hyde*. It was in *Sunrise*, though, that the cameraman really came into his own as a creative artist: Charles Rosher and Karl Struss, both portraitists and both stamped with the same attitude to cinema, together created a work dazzling in its innocent enchantment, creating a whole romantic world as complete as a Renoir's.

The sound period brought about a temporary lapse in the art of cinematography, the camera confined in giant boxes that could barely be moved (until Curtiz mounted them on wheels to give them greater mobility). Between two and five cameras photographed a scene, and the director monotonously cut from one camera to another. The photographer was often reduced to showing us a stage play from the point of view of someone in the front row of the stalls.

Yet a few cameramen, in some cases aided by their directors, did succeed in overcoming this crippling situation. Von Sternberg and Garmes created the rippling shadows and shining burnouses of *Morocco*, while Garmes's north light shone beautifully on the face of Dietrich. At Warners, Ernest Haller helped to establish a traditional low-key look in films of the calibre of Dieterle's *Scarlet Dawn*. Miraculously, cameras fought their way to movement: up a flight of stairs to follow a drunken Fredric March in *The Royal Family of Broadway*, travelling from a train through Penn Station to the station ceiling to take in a sudden flight of doves in Mamoulian's marvellous *Applause*. In *Transatlantic*, most creative of early sound films, Wong Howe had ceilings put on sets and used deep-focus shots ten years ahead of *Citizen Kane*, marvellously creating claustrophobia aboard a liner crossing the ocean.

As sound films improved and cameras were freed, cinematography reached its peak. Early colour films, now so foolishly discounted, had a delicate beauty seldom captured since: W. Howard Greene's soft landscapes of Ireland in *Wings of the Morning*, the quiet rural textures of James Wong Howe in *The Adventures of Tom Sawyer*, the glowing images of *Ramona*; all these led up to

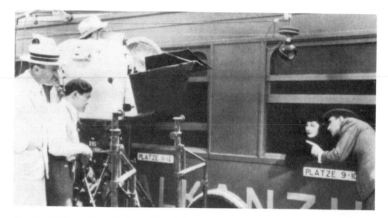

Stamboul Quest (1934): Sam Wood, James Wong Howe, Myrna Loy, George Brent

the wonderful first half of *Gone With the Wind*, in which Lee Garmes's soft and subtle colour evoked the Georgia of the past, and developed beautifully the three-colour Kalmus process first seen in *La Cucaracha* and *Becky Sharp* in the early thirties.

Black and white, too, became fully developed in that period. Lee Garmes's *Zoo in Budapest* (for Rowland V. Lee) still captivates: shot through delicate traceries of leaves and fronds, its images have a beauty untouched by time. Leon Shamroy's distinctive talent first emerged in *Private Worlds*, especially in the superb dramatic use of shadows in the hospital scenes, and in *You Only Live Once*, incomparably superior photographically to Lang's *Fury*, made shortly before and with a less individual cameraman. Victor Milner's work on Mamoulian's *Song of Songs* and Milestone's *The General Died at Dawn*, Karl Freund's work on *The Good Earth*, Charles Lang's on *A Farewell to Arms*: these were high points of the decade, and secured these cameramen's reputations in the sound period.

At Universal, Stanley Cortez was allowed to express his own personal attitudes to lighting in such extraordinary curios as *The Forgotten Woman*. At Warners, Ernest Haller, Sol Polito and Tony

Gaudio set their individual stamps on darkly realistic portraits of the American underworld. At Metro, there was less opportunity for creativity: Louis B. Mayer followed Cecil B. De Mille's precept that every detail on the screen should be seen with equal clarity, and the results were vapidly overpolished, save for the distinguished work of William Daniels and Karl Freund on *Camille*, the perpetuation of Garbo's image in Daniels's hands and Joseph Ruttenberg's breathtaking execution of Duvivier's *The Great Waltz*.

It was at the end of the thirties, and in the forties, that the most ravishing camerawork Hollywood has given us emerged. I have already remarked on Lee Garmes's images for *Gone With the Wind* (the chocolate-box colours of the second half, demanded by Selznick, were not as attractive even in the accomplished techniques of Ernest Haller). At Metro Joseph Ruttenberg, hitherto forced into a conventional mould while glamorizing the stars, brought a strong visual flavour to *Dr Jekyll and Mr Hyde*, *Gaslight* and *Waterloo Bridge*: a lacquered, solidly contrasty surface, particularly effective in scenes of street lamps shining through fog, Thames bridges ghostly against the black flow of the river, cloaked figures against shining cobbles. Much the same style was displayed in Harry Stradling's marvellous images for *The Picture of Dorian Gray*, and in Lucien Ballard's immaculate shooting of John Brahm's Victorian melodrama *The Lodger* at 20th Century-Fox, a studio notable for its images of a daguerreotype sharpness brilliantly executed by Arthur Miller, and for the flowing Technicolor seascapes and landscapes of its resident Delacroix, Leon Shamroy.

At R–K–O the greatest photography of the decade was seen, inspired by the enthusiasm of the young Orson Welles, in Gregg Toland's *Citizen Kane*, which developed techniques pioneered by Karl Struss and James Wong Howe to their fullest; in *The Magnificent Ambersons*, more fluent and graceful, a lasting testimonial to Cortez's genius; in Karl Struss's daring, underrated achievements in *Journey into Fear*, with its ingenious use of a ship blacked out in wartime. Nicholas Musuraca, scarcely inferior to these masters, delicately illuminated the films of Val Lewton, achieving his apotheosis in Siodmak's *The Spiral Staircase*, poetic, twilit, coolly elegant in its lighting style.

Universal and Paramount admittedly did little to develop the art of cinematography, though at Paramount Charles Lang shone and John F. Seitz's pitiless vein of realism made *Double Indemnity* and *The Lost Weekend* films of extraordinary visual distinction. Lee Garmes gave a luxuriant splendour to such disparate works as Dieterle's *The Searching Wind* and *Love Letters*, and Sol Polito, genius of Warner Brothers, arrived briefly to bring his uniquely fluent camera to bear on the excitements of *Sorry, Wrong Number*.

Warners was still the quintessential forties studio, creating, in its dark and glowing images, a whole nocturnal world of its own. Sol Polito's tracking shots, by far the most expert in Hollywood, gave a wonderful vivacity and pace to such films as Irving Rapper's *Rhapsody in Blue* and *The Adventures of Mark Twain*, and these biographies, together with Curtiz's *Mission to Moscow*, electrifyingly photographed by Bert Glennon, achieved the most stunning virtuoso tricks and effects in the cinema's history.

With the dire fifties came CinemaScope, and a collapse of visual quality even more disastrous than that which accompanied the dawn of sound. Shamroy, Garmes, Wong Howe and the other major figures complain bitterly to this day about the distortion, fuzziness and shallowness they were forced to provide us with in that period. Later, wide-screen techniques improved, 3-D had a mercifully brief life illuminated only by Peverell Marley's wonderfully eerie green-tinted street scenes in the rain for *House of Wax*, and Lee Garmes was able to achieve a high watermark of colour in *The Big Fisherman*. Joe MacDonald, already notable for his work with Ford (*My Darling Clementine*) and Wellman (*Yellow Sky*), Lucien Ballard, and Shamroy himself achieved some fine panoramas at 20th Century-Fox, home of the new system; and in VistaVision, with its splendid spherical lenses, William Daniels (*Strategic Air Command*) and Winton Hoch (*The Searchers*) provided images of superb depth and definition. Shamroy's sumptuous lighting for Tashlin's CinemaScope *The Girl Can't Help It* looked forward to his shining achievement of the sixties:

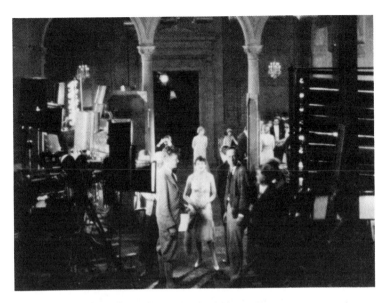

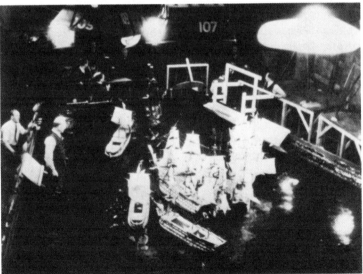

(*Above*) Karl Struss, in plus-fours, with director Joseph Henabery on the set of *Meet the Prince*, 1926; (*below*) the Armada scene in *Fire Over England*, 1936: cameraman, James Wong Howe

The Cardinal. And today Panavision, happily, has largely replaced CinemaScope.

In the last decade, we have seen the retirement or eclipse of many of the great veterans. Karl Struss and Ernest Haller have turned to commercials. Karl Freund, whose marvellous camerawork for Curtiz's story of the tobacco wars, *Bright Leaf* (1950), wrote a spectacular finis to his career in the cinema, is, alas, no longer with us. Joe MacDonald and Sol Polito are also dead. John ('North Light') Seitz, Charles Rosher, Arthur Miller and many others have retired for good. But it is comforting to know that many of the greatest veterans have been active, among them Charles Lang, Hal Mohr, Harry Stradling, Ted McCord and Russell Metty.

Stanley Cortez has moved from Wellesian fireworks through excursions into wild melodrama (*Black Tuesday, Shock Corridor*) towards the sweeping landscapes of *Blue* and the stark realism of *The Bridge at Remagen*. Wong Howe has given to *Hud* his special kind of bare naturalism and simplicity, achieving the finest effects of his career in the bleak truthfulness of *The Molly Maguires*, the setting of which is reminiscent of the mining town where he grew up. Garmes has given us the cool charm of *How to Save a Marriage*, bathing Stella Stevens in the north light that made the Dietrich face an unforgettable image more than thirty-five years ago. Leon Shamroy has splendidly splashed his paintbrush over the broad canvases of half a dozen epics. William Daniels's existence on the scene fifty years after *Foolish Wives* is in itself an astonishment.

And we have seen, in the past decade, the emergence of new cameramen with a revival of early film techniques, eschewing sets, shooting in all weathers and night for night, returning in fact with the advantage of new and faster film stock to the free and fresh ways of the early silent period. William Fraker (*The President's Analyst, Games, The Fox*), Philip Lathrop (*Point Blank, Finian's Rainbow, The Happening*), Haskell Wexler (*Who's Afraid of Virginia Woolf?, The Thomas Crown Affair*), and William Butler (*The Rain People*) are among the new generation of cameramen who dislike the academic formalist approach of many of their elders, who prefer an informal realism even more radical than Wong Howe's. Now that, as Stanley Cortez remarks, 'black and white is dead', we are clearly in for a period of naturalism in colour (flawed, one hopes, not too deeply by the decline in print standards). The influence of French cameramen like Coutard and Decaë is an obvious one. But there is still room for the veterans; and this book is a testimony to their individual skills.

In transcribing these taped interviews, I have striven to preserve the eccentric, quirky tone of the subjects, whose tone of voice has a vigour, a grassroots American honesty and lack of polish, it would be a shame to sandpaper in transmission. I am proud to name them my personal friends, finding every new encounter with them more refreshingly unpredictable than the last: Leon Shamroy, gruff as a Russian bear, startlingly similar to the even gruffer Josef von Sternberg, living in a house as spectacularly cluttered as any set in *Justine*; Lee Garmes, married to the lovely Ruth Hall, charming leading lady to Eddie Cantor and the Marx Brothers, a gentle-hearted proud teddy-bear of a man in a duplex as delicately fastidious as a doll's house; James Wong Howe, said to be terrible-tempered on the set, but in his quietly elegant hillside home the most gently lovable of Chinese sages; Stanley Cortez, powerfully built and handsomely tanned in a Valentino Spanish villa, looking every inch the matinée idol figure his brother Ricardo Cortez was to millions of female fans, his hair untouched by grey and his face that of a man twenty years younger, genial, mischievous and charmingly maddening; Arthur Miller, pottering round the American Society of Cinematographers building, where Conway Tearle once lived (and grew the palms that decorated Pola Negri's boat in *Bella Donna*); Karl Struss, at eighty monumentally tall, slow-speaking and kindly, one of the few men who could soothe the savage brow of Cecil B. De Mille; William Daniels, cool, neat as a chemist in exquisitely fine-cut rimless spectacles.

Here are these men's stories, told by themselves: from their sources of light, the images that have haunted many of us for half a lifetime have sprung and flourished.

1: Leon Shamroy

What's the nature of this thing anyhow? There are no great cameramen. And you can't be objective about yourself. It would be better if you spoke to my assistant, or somebody else. Wouldn't it?

My father was a Russian, who graduated from the University of Moscow. One of his younger brothers was a revolutionary and had to leave the country, and became a doctor in America. My father, who was a chemist, came over to see him, about 1889, and liked it so much he decided to stay. He took his degree at Columbia.

He built a drugstore and threw out the soda-fountain. He thought it was a mistake in a pharmacy! I myself wanted to be an engineer. My three uncles were all engineers and went to Dresden Polytechnic. Often on Saturdays and Sundays after a week of high school I'd work in one of these uncles' offices as a junior draughtsman on a new type of air-cooled radio motor. It was called the Lawrence motor and subsequently became the Wright Whirlwind Motor.

The remuneration in engineering was so sparse that I started looking around for other fields. We had some cousins who became affiliated with Griffith and I helped with the laboratory work. Other members of the family migrated out here. So I came and got a job in a laboratory, and I thought with my vanity that I'd knock 'em for a loop, but instead there came thirteen years of struggle and starvation.

I began making experimental films. I did them for nothing on speculation. I had no proper equipment and I used about a couple of lights. B. P. Schulberg of Paramount finally saw them and sent for me. He signed me up in 1932. I was broke; I had squandered my money on poor, starving girls, whisky, and so on. The first of my experimental films was made with a Hungarian called Paul Fejos. It was called *The Last Moment*. I promoted 4,000 dollars and the stage space for it, arranged laboratory work, and everything. It was the first silent picture made without any explanatory titles, it was all done in subjective camera. It got rave reviews.

Fejos was a very charming guy but a charlatan. He double-crossed me. When the picture was shown and everyone liked it, Carl Laemmle signed us up as a team but Fejos deliberately left me out in the cold. He shunned me completely, even though I had contributed so much, and I was literally starving because of this. But you know what a Hungarian is like; you know the story: two Hungarians are learning about how to make an omelette, and the first one says to the second, 'How shall we go about it?' And the second says, 'First I steal two eggs.' And that sums up Paul Fejos.

I made a picture called *The Tell-Tale Heart* from Edgar Allan Poe, in one day. It was directed by Charles Klein, a German cameraman, who didn't do too well, so I reshot it. I never got any credit.

Then I did something called *Blindfold*, or *In The Fog*. These pictures at least had the merit of getting me to the attention of the right people, and my camerawork was described as worth its weight in gold, a rare thing in those days. John M. Stahl, for whom I later shot *Leave Her to Heaven*, saw *The Last Moment* and said, 'The guy is great, but he's dangerous.' He thought I was too artistic.

I went to Mexico somewhere around that period and did something for Flaherty on an ancient Indian tribe. It was called *Acoma, The Sky City*. It showed their customs, and how they still propitiated the gods to get a fair shake in life. They lived on top of a huge rock . . . unfortunately the producers started to introduce a love-story and all that shit. Flaherty and I rebelled. And then to

The Last Moment (1928): vision by Pierrot (Otto Mattiesen) of himself at bedside of dying wife→

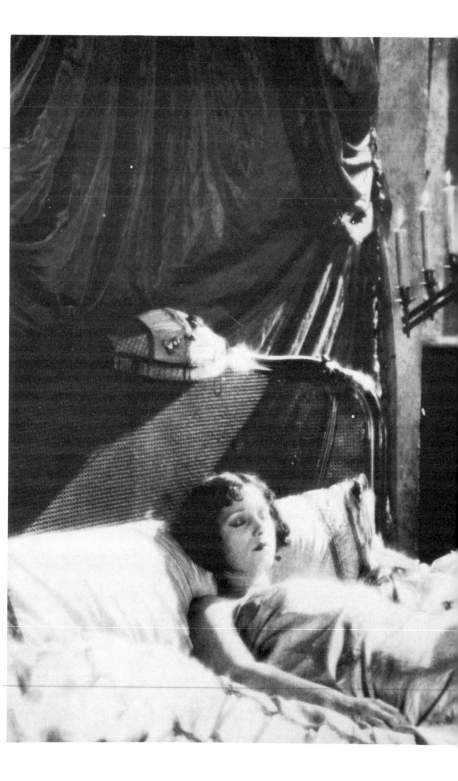

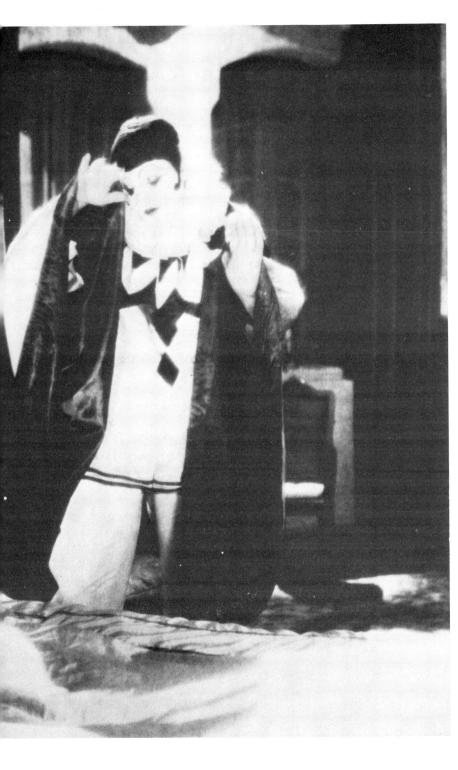

cap everything there was a fire in a warehouse that destroyed the print. It nearly killed me; all the work I had done was gone. Eight months, and my young heart was spent on it. Then, I recall, while we were in Tucson after we'd shot the Indians, Murnau came in to the hotel and talked to Flaherty about forming a company to go to the South Seas, to make a film. I didn't have enough money to go with them, as I only had fifteen dollars after I had paid my ten-dollar union fee. Instead, I made a two-reel documentary based on an Indian legend . . . I've forgotten the name, and it was never released.

Harry Cohn hired me, saying I was the greatest genius in Hollywood, then fired me five days later. They changed their minds almost right away because, as Sam Briskin, who was Cohn's right-hand man, told me, they weren't ready for artistic people yet. They weren't going to be M–G–M, they made commercial pictures. Fadeout. Years later, Schulberg lent me to Columbia to make *Private Worlds*, a picture about psychiatry, in the mid 1930s (the reason was Colbert wanted me; I had shot her in *Three-Cornered Moon*). They admired my work; they had completely forgotten they fired me years before!

After the Flaherty disaster and the Columbia visit, I worked for Jack Cummings, a producer who was Louis B. Mayer's nephew. I did for him pictures that were parodies of the famous screen epics, starring dogs. They were very popular. The dogs looked so realistic when we were making *All Quiet on the Canine Front* that when they were mown down with imitation bullets the Humane Society complained!

After that, I left for an ethnological expedition to the Orient to prepare some filmed material. We were two days out of Yokohama on the 'Empress of Canada' when I called my chow boy for breakfast one morning; I called him at seven and by twelve and a few Haig and Haigs later he still hadn't come. So I thought, what the hell's happened to him, and I opened the door, and I saw him lying dead in a pool of blood. It was the worst thing that ever happened on a ship on the Pacific: somebody had run amok and stabbed thirty people to death. We were scared to death. They found the man with thirty-five knives in his bed; a Filipino in fourth class. The whole ship was put under surveillance, but I managed to walk off it with a camera and 100,000 feet of film completely undetected.

I travelled all through Japan in 1930 and shot some marvellous footage including the harbour, which I wasn't supposed to do. I became very enamoured of the Japanese, they were very loyal, very trustworthy, and I don't know what the hell we had a war with them about. I left Japan with the footage – I was afraid to ship it out – and somehow survived the interrogation from the military when I left. They followed me into China, perhaps because they were afraid I would give installations secrets to the Chinese; in China I travelled fourth class on a train; you can imagine the filthy stench. I shot and shot, and sneaked the film out. I got stuff on China you can't imagine; if they'd found out I would have been strung up.

When I finally got to Manila I kissed the ground. I literally got down on my knees and thanked God I was safe; I mean it. And when I had showered and shaved and had tiffin at the Hotel Manila, I opened a paper and read that the same guy who had run amok on the ship had just been stabbed to death. All that stood me in good stead later, when I shot a picture called *Crash Dive*, with Tyrone Power. We were trying to get permission to use the Newport Naval Base at the end of the picture and a naval captain discussed it with us. We were at a club and while Tyrone Power danced with his daughter I told him of my experience back in 1930, and it turned out he had been on the same ship, and he was so tickled he gave us permission to use the base.

I went on to the Dutch East Indies – the first guy in there with a motion-picture sound camera. I did Bali, Samarai, Batavia, and in World War II all the material was presented to Washington, and the War Department thanked me for my efforts. They had all the material they needed for bombing targets.

I went on to make quickies, serials, and then I worked for Paramount on contract. In those early days, of course, no matter what the historians say, almost everything in the dialogue sections

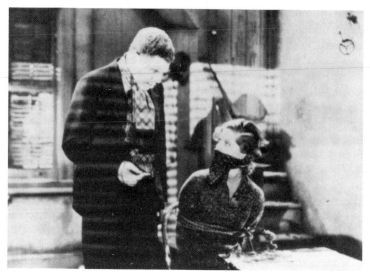

Soak the Rich: Lionel Stander, Mary Taylor

was just 'photographed play'. *Three-Cornered Moon*, for instance; my first with Claudette Colbert, who liked me. And several films with Marion Gering. My signature became established as high-contrast: they'd always say, 'use more light', but I liked shadows. A lot of fellows could recognize my work straight away, no matter who was directing.

Private Worlds, directed by Gregory La Cava, with Claudette and with Charles Boyer, was a film about mental illness, years ahead of its time. I used zoom lenses in that long before they were popular, such as the scene when Big Boy Williams, a patient, goes berserk. Nobody used zooms then; there were only two in existence. You didn't have light-meters for them, to judge the light correctly. You couldn't see what you were doing.

Soak the Rich, the Hecht-MacArthur picture I did, was a flop. They didn't release it, they were afraid of it. I co-directed it; they wanted to give me 250 bucks less a week in return for billing as co-director. It was the story of the richest man in the world who endows a college rather like UCLA, and his daughter becomes enamoured of the young leader of the student body. There was a good deal about politics. I recall the character of the butler, who in answer to the question 'What is Communism?' said, 'Communism is the growing pains of the young.'

We shot most of *You Only Live Once* at night. We were shooting in the old siding at Highland Avenue where you can still see the railway tracks, and Walter Wanger was getting impatient. At two o'clock one morning, Fritz Lang sent me to Wanger with the message, 'You're breaking my heart.' And Wanger said, 'You're not only breaking my heart, but my bankroll.' Lang was fantastically meticulous, like one of those artists who would paint over and over again on the same canvas, covering one painting with another. He *is* an artist, but in this business you have to be practical as well. You're always limited by the mass audience.

We worked every night until three o'clock, and Hank Fonda had just got married! We'd work every shot out in such detail . . . I'd tape it from mark to mark, and at seven in the morning Lang would be back again after only four hours away, a long drive and maybe two hours sleep, and he'd say to me that the shot I'd prepared at that fantastic early morning hour wouldn't work: 'It hasn't,' he'd put it in his German accent, 'the possibility.' I was furious. I always believed that the audience didn't care about all those finicky details he insisted upon; that all you needed was to be an impressionist, to create an illusion, a mood, that matched the way the characters were thinking. He didn't agree.

I wanted the picture to end differently. After the police machine-gunned these two enemies of society I wanted the camera to dolly in to a close shot of a little baby burping, and the title 'You Only Live Once'. But Wanger wouldn't listen.

That was the story of *Bonnie and Clyde* before its time . . . romantic, though, not realistic. Burnett Guffey was my assistant at the time, incidentally. I told him how much I liked *Bonnie and Clyde* photographically, and he thought it was lousy. And of course if you analysed it shot by shot it stank. But the backgrounds

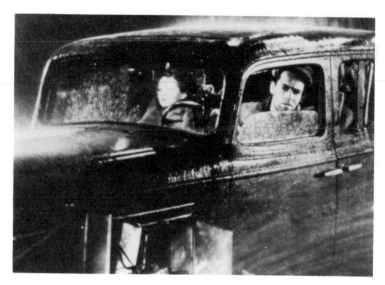

You Only Live Once: 'the story of *Bonnie and Clyde* before its time' . . . Sylvia Sidney, Henry Fonda

were great . it was like Henri Cartier-Bresson, journalistic photography that told the story. Rough, but that was right for it.

I left Paramount when B. P. Schulberg fell from grace and was practically blackballed from the industry in the late thirties. Then Selznick sent for me to make a test for Janet Gaynor. I didn't want to do it, but I finally agreed, then I got a shock. I discovered that the test was being used competitively; that tests were being done of her by other cameramen, by Karl Struss for instance – who, they said, took twelve hours – to see which cameraman they liked best. I took twenty minutes with my test, and they were astonished. The result was that Selznick engaged me to do Janet's picture *The Young in Heart.*

I was living at the old Kelton Hotel – 75 dollars a month and food – with my wife, when I got a call to come to Selznick's house on a Sunday. We ran the picture – it was shot in an unorthodox, realistic style – and Selznick started delivering a lecture, 'Where is

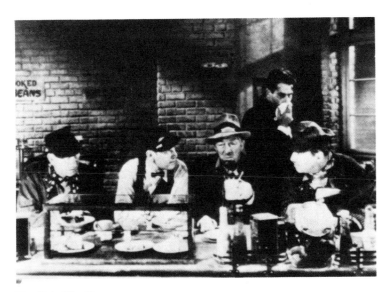

You Only Live Once

the daring of Lee Garmes? . . .' And I gave it to him quick: I told him he had engaged me and he'd have to let me do things my way. The result was he left me to my own devices and I was the only cameraman who did two pictures for him in a row. In the end I became a good friend of his and Jennifer's, and I did the tests for Jennifer that got her the part in *Song of Bernadette*.

Myron Selznick got me my job at 20th, but thereby cut me out of being cameraman on *Gone With The Wind*. They got Lee Garmes instead, but he'll never see the day he's as good as I am, and that goes for anybody in the motion-picture business. Then they fired Lee and tried to get me back but I couldn't come.

Zanuck gave me complete freedom at 20th. I was my own master there. Here I developed my technique of using the absolute minimum of lights on a set. I'd always say, 'God was a great photographer. He'd only gotten one light.' To light economically is a rarity in this business: most cameramen put a light in front, others

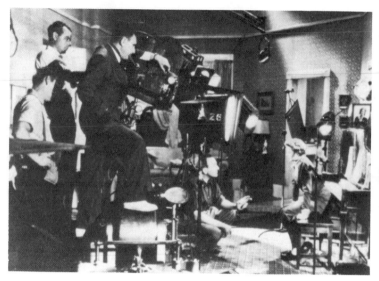

You Only Live Once: Fritz Lang directs Sylvia Sidney; Leon Shamroy with arm on camera

at the sides, fix up backlighting here and there; I don't. For instance, on *Justine*, in the scene with Michael York telephoning Justine in the bedroom, I only had one light shining on his face – to suggest dawn – and two other small lights. Every light has to mean something, be fully justified, like words in a sentence.

I think one drawback in my many years at 20th was that I became too slick, too polished; everything started to look like magazine illustrations with those gelatins I was using. I had an argument with the studio on my first colour picture for them, *Down Argentine Way*. They wanted softer colour, but I wanted it hard and bright, and it came out as sharp as a tack. I did other colour musicals for them; and then *Roxie Hart* in black and white in the middle. That wasn't so hard to do because my technique was twenties' technique anyway! *Wilson* I was very proud of; Ernest Palmer started it, but Zanuck took him off after a week: Darryl had been spoilt by my style. I ran the picture up here recently for

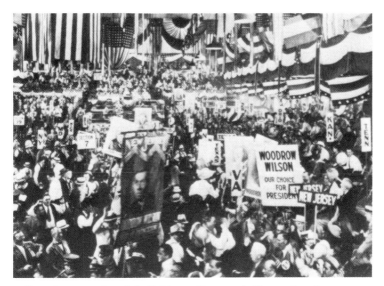

Wilson: the re-creation of the Baltimore Democratic Convention of 1912

Henry King, and it's still great, but it was a pacifist picture when war was on, they couldn't show it to the troops, and making it was a mistake.

I used natural interiors for that – very rare in those days. We did one scene in the Shrine Ballroom, and I went down and hid lights behind the flags, and did a complete floor map so as to work out how we could move the arcs around. I had a hundred men moving the arcs around, and each man had to be handpicked. I went down at four o'clock in the morning of the day we were going to shoot and turned on every one of the arcs for Henry King. He was astounded at the effect it gave, and when we showed the first long shots to Zanuck, his staff cheered and Zanuck kissed me. It's the most startling shot I've ever done, the most startling shot I've ever seen on the screen. Five thousand people in a blaze of light, with the flags flapping, a re-creation of the Baltimore Democratic Convention in 1912.

In *Forever Amber* I matched the title by using amber-colour gelatins. I shot all the exteriors, or many of them, in actual rain. I wanted a dull, monotonous effect, and I used liquid smoke hovering over the bodies when they painted the doors red to indicate the presence of plague. I showed smoke coming out from the doors to indicate something sinister inside. There was something strange about that picture: Linda Darnell was burned in the Great Fire of London, and in *Anna and the King of Siam* she was burned to death as a punishment, and then, it's extraordinary, she actually died in a fire. . . . And she only just escaped death in the picture, because during the Great Fire a roof caved in, I pulled the camera back and she just got out with it in time. She was terrified of fire, almost as though she had a premonition.

I won the *Look* Award for *Twelve O'Clock High*. I gave it the appearance of England in Florida locations, and – again long before this became fashionable – I used actual huts for the interiors, avoiding studio. For instance, there is a famous shot of the air force men around a table, looking at a map, and we didn't fake the shot or use a set at all, we left the low hut ceiling in, everything. In *Prince of Foxes* I again used an actual place: a palace was the only set in the picture, everything else was done in the buildings where the action would have occurred. We went to the Castel San'Angelo, San Gimignano, many other places. I used the Palazzo Municipale in Siena . . .

Then came the terrible days of CinemaScope. Those early Bausch and Lomb lenses were hell; and the films became very granulated. We've never had the sharpness we had in the old technically wonderful days of three-colour Technicolor; just compare the work I did then, it's not that it's better, just better shown off by the processing. It nearly drove me out of my mind, seeing what happened to my work when it was spread out all over that screen. I fought to get Panavision introduced on the Fox lot, and at last I won. It does help; in some ways it's very good. But those wide-screen 'revolutions': oh my God! You got a stage play again, you put pictures back to the earliest sound days, and you couldn't even do close-ups, because they'd distort so horribly. But

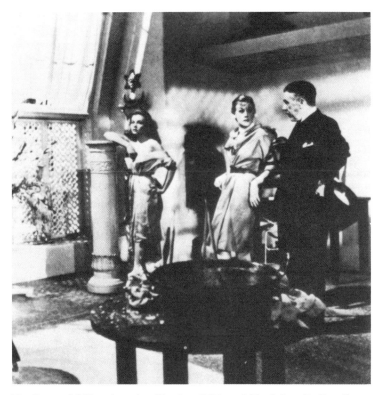

The Snows of Kilimanjaro: Ava Norring, Hildegard Knef, Leo G. Carroll

though it wrecked the art of film for a decade, wide screen saved the picture business.

Just before the horror started, I got through a picture I'm very proud of: *Snows of Kilimanjaro.* Almost every foot of it was shot in the studio, even those night shots under the mountain, some of the best stuff ever done, and nobody guessed for a moment it wasn't all taking place in Africa. Charles G. Clarke did the few shots of Kilimanjaro itself. *The Egyptian* was also all Hollywood; it would have been better if Marlene Dietrich had been playing the old hooker, the old whore. And Marlon Brando should have been the man; but he hated Mike Curtiz, he disliked Bella Darvi and he wasn't too fond of the script.

I enjoyed making *Daddy Long Legs*; like its director, Jean Negulesco, it was underrated, and Roland Petit's dance numbers were wonderful. Jean's had a rough time; this youth thing they have here has pushed him out. A tragedy: he has a great talent. *South Pacific* I remember with less pleasure; I did all those colour filter effects against my better judgment. I went over to Tahiti to scout locations, and when I did a tidal wave hit the island. I walked through the slush, and I decided to do a lot of the film in driving rain, musical numbers and all. Then I wanted to bring in an effect I had seen after I came back from the Orient in 1930, travelling through the Straits of Messina, when Etna was erupting; it turned amber and green and red and lavender. I went to Fiji and shot the opening credits the way I wanted to, in subdued natural colours, the real colours of the tropics. I wanted to do 'Bali Ha'i' with tropical realism and animation effects, but they wouldn't hear of it at Fox, and worse than that they used a painted backdrop for Bali Ha'i instead of the real place I wanted to show. It was awful. The mauves and purples were horribly overdone; I wrote Logan a letter about a thing called 'restraint'. Three years later my assistant was in Paris and he ran into Logan on the Champs-Elysées, and Logan said, 'Tell Leon he was right. It wasn't a critical success, that picture. But also tell him I made 3,000,000 dollars out of it.'

Cleopatra was an awful tough business; it nearly killed me. There was no script, you never knew what they were doing from day to day, and I had to take over from Jack Hildyard, who did the Mamoulian footage. I saw some of the Mamoulian stuff; I thought it was terrible. There were one or two good photographic moments in my version – when Rex Harrison has a fit, for instance. But as for the rest!

By contrast with *Cleopatra*, which dragged on for months, *The Cardinal* came in under fifty-three days. The only bad thing about the picture was that the boy was no good. I wanted Brad Dillman, but they wouldn't have him.

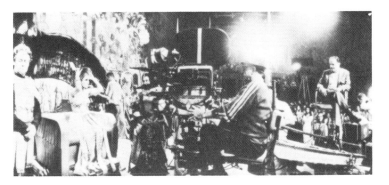

Cleopatra: Shamroy behind camera, Joseph L. Mankiewicz seated right

My biggest recent challenge was *The Agony and the Ecstasy*. As always, I wanted complete realism; so I shot the Sistine ceiling with almost nowhere to hide the lights, none behind the camera possible, one behind a panel, others on the floor . . . and we were working from a spot seventy feet above the ground. It was a polished film, but *Planet of the Apes* was very rough. It was done in Arizona, in a place where there's no way to get in except by helicopter, and when you arrive there are only a few feet to manœuvre in. It was a good challenge and, of course, I enjoyed shooting those cramped interiors of the ape city. That's what I like best: solving problems – where to hide lights, how to get an authentic look. In *Justine*, I've stripped every bit of gloss from my style. It has been so 'realistic' making it, it nearly killed me!

A problem I had on *Justine* was over my conception of true colour. I believe in accuracy; if you walk into a room with a candle flame, only the area round the flame should have warm colour; the rest of it should be cold. But Cukor wanted the whole scene to be warm, through the use of coloured filters. I remember when I was making *The Black Swan*, I wanted to dispense with the usual Technicolor man from Kalmus, and to emulate the old masters, men like Van Dyck and Rembrandt, and I'd say to Zanuck, 'When you're shooting a sunset, use yellow light instead of white light,

33

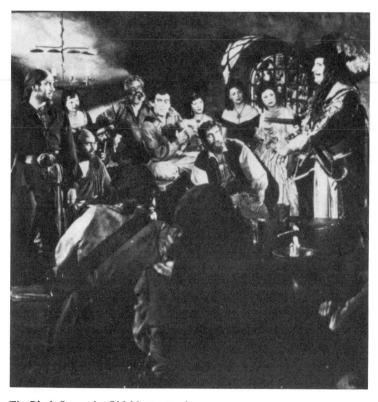

The Black Swan: the Old Master touch

and ignore realism, make a deliberate mistake.* And Mrs Kalmus went to see Zanuck and said, 'That isn't the way a colour picture should be photographed.' Zanuck stepped on me, but I still was the first black and white man to win an Oscar for colour – with that picture. And every picture I ever made should have won an Oscar as well, especially *Snow White and the Three Stooges.* Have a cigar?

2: Lee Garmes

A cameraman is often the chief in a film. His lighting can be the main factor in its success. Very few directors know anything about the uses of light. Von Sternberg knew a great deal, but even he couldn't see the necessity for the balance of light and shadow in a shot. In most cases, the director leaves me to my own devices. I don't like photography to *steal* a scene, when the scene is an important one. But sometimes you get a scene that is not very interesting. Then I try to get something that is very beautiful and startling, to increase the interest.

You can follow my style like a thread through many directors' films. Ever since I began, Rembrandt has been my favourite artist. I've always used his technique of north light – of having my main source of light on a set always coming from the north. He used to have a great window in his studio ceiling or at the end of the room which always caught that particular light. And of course I've always followed Rembrandt in my fondness for low key. If you look at his paintings, you'll see an awful lot of blacks. No strong highlights. You'll see faces and you'll see hands and portions of clothing he specifically wants you to notice, but he'll leave other details to your imagination. Of course, film is transparent material, unlike canvas, and sometimes too much light gets through it, and you are apt to see things I might not want you to see. But I like to highlight significant detail, and I have been able to do this in spite of a great variety of directors. For instance, in *An American*

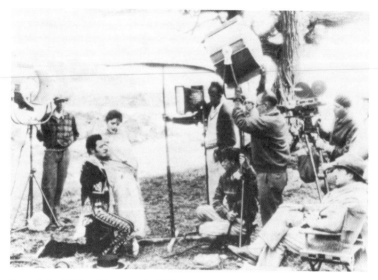

Rose of the Golden West (1927): Gilbert Roland and Mary Astor; George Fitzmaurice in director's chair, Lee Garmes in beret: shooting on location at Monterey with portable generators for light

Tragedy I used north light in the courtroom. All the light came from that north window.

During my childhood I lived in Denver, Colorado. After dinner at the end of the day my family and I would play 'movies'. We'd see these big signboards of motion pictures, things like that, and we would try to reproduce the scenes accurately, with our antics. It was my role to play cameraman. I found a couple of orange boxes or apple boxes and nailed them together and then I discovered an old hand-wringer in a junkyard that the women used to use to wring out their clothes. I nailed it to the top of the boxes and as the others played their scenes I would crank this wringer like a camera. Little did I know that one day years later I would become a cinematographer!

My father was a horticulturist. He and my mother were divorced when I was quite young, and my grandmother raised me. We moved out here to California in September 1916, and I got a job as a painter's assistant in the paint department at the old Thomas H. Ince Studios. Henry Hathaway and I were property boys together, at Inceville, where Sunset Boulevard comes into the ocean. It was formerly a ranch, the 101 Bison Ranch, where they had a lot of buffalo. The New York Motion Picture Company had leased this land and put Tom Ince in charge of it. Then, later on, Harry Culver at Culver City gave Ince the land where M–G–M is now.

I got to know a German cameraman called John Leezer who made the first picture in soft focus. He had gauze over the lens for the whole film. Billy Bitzer, Griffith's cameraman, saw what John was doing and he started using it. He often got credit for soft focus, but Leezer was the originator. I worked with Leezer for a year and a half.

I got my first job doing slapstick comedies for Gale Henry. I was paid the sum of fifty dollars a week, which was quite a bit of money at that time – the end of World War I. We had no lights; we had to light the sets on the open stages with reflectors, catching the sunlight. I learned my trade bit by bit, taking hard knocks on the way; I got my most valuable experience at FBO, the Film Booking Office, where Malcolm St Clair was a very 'hot' young director, who had been with Mack Sennett. There was a story called *Fighting Blood* then being serialized in a national magazine, about a small-town prize-fighter who would meet a different fighter every week, and like Perry Mason never lose a fight. We made thirty-six of these two-reelers with Mal as director, and for each episode I would experiment with a different type of lighting. It was all very good experience for me for the future, because I knew if I got into a picture I had to go like lightning or go slowly and meticulously according to the subject.

As for close-ups, I didn't really learn that craft until *The Grand Duchess and The Waiter*, a feature I did for Mal. It was my first feature film at the Paramount Studios. We did the whole picture in tones of grey; the sets and the furniture alike. The studio wasn't happy with it, and sent it to New York, which returned it and asked for certain retakes. We saw the film again and said, 'Jeez, we don't know what the hell to do.' We tried, and even then they held it up till Christmas week because 'people would get cold and go to see anything.' When the picture was released, every critic gave it the most wonderful, glowing reviews. The studio couldn't understand why such a rotten picture got good reviews, but it turned out to be one of Paramount's top money-making pictures of the year. Which proved that the management didn't know as much as the people making the films. After that Mal was the fair-haired boy again, and Adolphe Menjou and Florence Vidor became stars.

I made a couple of pictures with Mal and Menjou in New York. There I met Rex Ingram. Later I worked on a number of pictures with him in Nice, at his kind invitation. I was sorry to leave Mal, of course: he was a fine artist, he could draw very well, he had a lot of feeling, a sensitive person. The big success he had suddenly might have gone to his head, because he came in a little late occasionally, he was a bit eccentric in that respect, but he made good pictures . . . finally he got into trouble with some remarks he made at Paramount that were not intended to be taken seriously, but were enough to have him ostracized. By the way, he helped Darryl Zanuck in the early stages – we used to call Darryl 'gopher' because of his protruding teeth – Mal bought his first story, *Havoc*, and got him writing credits.

Ingram was a perfectionist, who kept hounding me and hounding me to follow the style of John F. Seitz, who had been with him before; Johnny didn't use any rim-lights or backlights, anything like that. He had a north-light effect on his faces, and Rex wanted that; I gave it to him, and I fell in love with north light, and used it as my signature. Only Johnny, Vic Milner and I were using the north light; we put it on the map. Like Mal, Rex was a painter, and understood what I was doing. I started off by doing *The Garden of Allah* for him; Alice Terry was fine, and I loved working with them.

I started work for Alexander Korda not long afterwards. He was extremely creative, but he was more of a promoter than anything else. We were close personal friends and associates for many years, starting with *The Private Life of Helen of Troy*. He had no

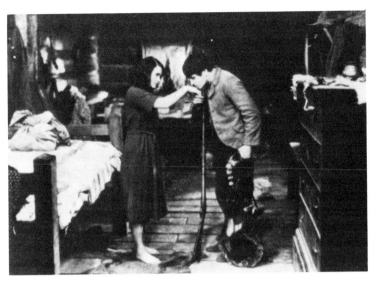

The Little Shepherd of Kingdom Come: Richard Barthelmess, Molly O'Day

knowledge of lighting; he was interested only in the story and the acting. Maria Korda looked excellent in north light. The picture was a semi-spectacle; not bad. We had all the Venice canal scenes bathed in yellow light, with the players in white.

One extraordinary feature of Alfred Santell's *Little Shepherd of Kingdom Come,* which I made for First National, was that they had Richard Barthelmess, who was an adult of course, play in the opening scene a boy of six years old! He was in his late thirties at the time. We used Mazda lights on that one; I think I was the first to make a full Mazda light picture, without arcs, just naked bulbs and lead sheets to bump the light off where I wanted it to go. I was offered a partnership in Mazda lights after that; foolishly I didn't take one, or I would be a very wealthy man today. They are a multi-million dollar company now.

I had first used Mazda lights on a John Leezer picture with Dorothy Gish; they wanted me to shoot a scene with a little white mouse, after they had all gone home. It had to sit up on its tiny legs and sort of wash its face. I knew if I used arc-lights the carbons would burn down and just at the time I'd got the mouse to sit up the carbon would flare out and scare the little animal. So I found two or three blue Mazda bulbs around and stuck them up; that was good. It was a nice shot, and from that time many cameramen started to make pictures without arcs, but with simple bulbs instead.

I came into the sound period with Al Jolson in *Say It With Songs*, which I liked, and with George Arliss on *Disraeli*. At the time we were making *Disraeli*, Warners were using five or six cameras, but Al Green, the director, and I cut them down to one or two, thus helping the whole industry. The big icehouse cameras were terrible bugaboos to work with. Mike Curtiz helped out by mounting them on a chassis with Ford axles and tyres, and a finder on the side. Then he added a turntable; this was quite revolutionary. He was very enterprising.

For Goldwyn I made *Whoopee*, but later we agreed to disagree on a Ronald Colman picture, and parted. My agent got me the job on *Morocco*; Jo von Sternberg was just back from Germany, he was young, and feeling his way. We had a supervisor on the picture called Hector Turnbull who had something to do with the script of *Morocco*; he was what was called a producer later. I recall once Jo drove me back from the Paramount ranch where we were shooting, and Hector bawled the hell out of both of us; he told us we were going well over schedule, over budget. Jo didn't have much to say, so I said, 'Hector, we're making a good picture; you can see that, can't you?' He admitted, 'Yes.' And I told him this was going to be something special, and that in a few months he was going to come and apologize to us. He did; and he congratulated us for defying him.

Unfortunately I didn't have sufficient time to make tests of Marlene Dietrich; I had seen *The Blue Angel*, and, based on that, I lit her with a sidelight, a half-tone, so that one half of her face was bright and the other half was in shadow. I looked at the first day's work and I thought, 'My God, I can't do this, it's exactly

40

Shanghai Express: Clive Brook and Dietrich

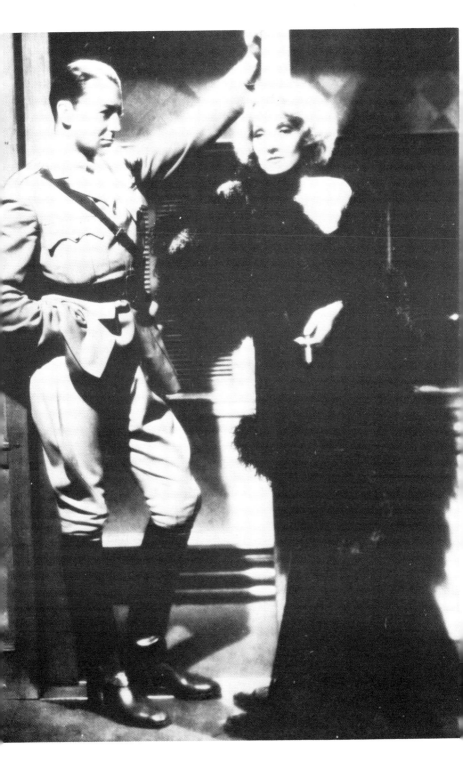

what Bill Daniels is doing with Garbo.' We couldn't, of course, have two Garbos! So, without saying anything to Jo, I changed to the north-light effect. He had no suggestions for changes, he went ahead and let me do what I wanted. The Dietrich face was my creation.

He left the lighting to me at all times. He was very particular about one thing only: sets. Sometimes to suit a setting he would ask me to do something special: in *An American Tragedy* he wanted the figures in a house to be in silhouette against moonlight, to show that a particular garden he had designed himself was fully pictorial. It worked out startlingly well. On *Morocco*, we had lattice-work in the streets; we shot at his suggestion at high noon for some interesting rippling shadows. Quite a lot of the picture was done in natural sunlight, rare at the time. The night scenes were shot at the Paramount ranch, and I did some of the best close-ups of Marlene Dietrich against a white wall there; it was artificially lit to simulate daylight. She still likes to have the north light to this day. She had a great mechanical mind, and knew the camera. She would always stop in the exact position that was right for her.

Dishonoured was a great spy story, and Jo did a beautiful job; but it wasn't 'box-office'. My favourite picture with Jo was *Shanghai Express*, which won me the Academy Award. The big train was put on a spare branch line in Chatswood, out in the San Fernando Valley. Hans Dreier built a magnificent set of a town and Jo told him to make it as close to the train as possible, with only one or two inches clearance, in fact. When the train came through for the first trial it hit a building and had to stop or it would have knocked the whole set down! We converted San Bernardino railroad station and painted the train white for the final arrival scene. I had a favourite shot of Marlene Dietrich when she pulled the door close and leant her head against the wall and looked up: I just had an inky-dinky spot directly over her head, that's all. And I used that again when she stood at the back of the train. Things like that won me the Oscar.

The opening of Howard Hawks's *Scarface* ran 1,000 feet, and

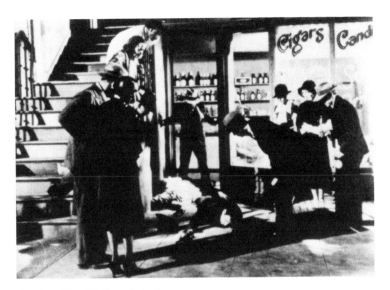

Scarface: North light and shadows

we shot it the first day, travelling through the streamers at the end
of a party scene. Originally, the picture ended differently: the
censors of the time didn't like it. As we had it, the smoke filled the
room, when Scarface the gangster is trapped in the house, and he
went down and outside. We showed the police riddling him with
bullets, and he fell into a big pile of horse manure, where he
belonged. The censor didn't like that, they wanted something
different, so we did it over again. I wanted the picture full of bare
light bulbs, dating from my work on *Little Shepherd*: I hung these
low, and through my use of the north-light effect the images were
full of shadows, of my particular kind of shadows.

Rowland V. Lee's *Zoo in Budapest* was a very big challenge to
me, and it shot Loretta Young to stardom. With the aid of a
gardener I knew, I went out and bought tall, short and medium-
sized lacy plants, all we could find; and I placed these things in
front of the camera for every composition. I hid telephone-poles

with bamboo tied together with wire; the whole picture gave the impression of taking place in a rich tracery of leaves and fronds and stalks. Extraordinary.

At about the same time I did *Smilin' Through*, with Norma Shearer, directed by Sidney Franklin. She had a slight cast in one eye, but she'd always say, 'Lee, if you see me going cross-eyed, watch for me.' I'd give her a cue: I'd stop the camera and say, loudly, something like, 'A light went out.' And I'd fiddle around a bit until she'd blink a signal at me and she could finish the shot. *Strange Interlude* – also with her – was a problem, because you had to keep the camerawork pretty static while the characters delivered their thoughts in full. It was very dull.

It was in the early thirties that my association with Ben Hecht and Charlie MacArthur began. The partnership, which led to *The Scoundrel*, started through Selznick: David knew me because he had been over at Paramount working with Schulberg when I was there. He fell in love with my work, and when Ben Hecht started to come into independent production, David recommended me. It was a wonderful partnership, and I became a half-ass producer and director with them. Financially the association with them hurt me; professionally it helped me.

Crime Without Passion had a good story by Ben and Charlie MacArthur. They brought in a stage designer who built everything to the proscenium, with bedrooms forty feet wide and twenty feet high; so I said, it won't work, let's thank him and say goodbye. I redid the sets myself with a construction man, to bring the bedroom down to ten by twelve, and make all the other sets the proper size too.

We had to add a night-club scene. We had run out of money, as the scene hadn't been budgeted for, so I created the whole thing out of a few drapes and bits of cellophane, a couple of chairs and a table, and a little tiny stage. It cost exactly twenty dollars to create. I directed about 60–70 per cent of the picture; we'd start at nine a.m. and some days Hecht was there, some days MacArthur; they'd start working on the picture at eleven a.m.! So they relied on me. They set the style of how they wanted the dialogue done, and I would direct the whole physical side of it.

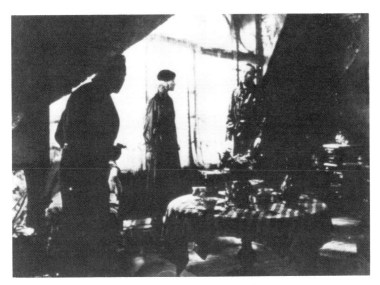

The Scoundrel: Stanley Ridges, Julie Haydon, Noël Coward

I experimented in the courtroom scene as well. That was built in sections; a *whole* set was never built. I just did the judge's bench, the window, a bit of wall, the witness stand, the table for the attorneys, and every one of these was on wheels; I'd wheel them around, and when I moved one out of the way I'd put another section in its place, and rearrange the lights accordingly. It saved an awful lot of money. The north light gave the whole thing a look of three-dimensional reality, without a single comprehensive long shot of the courtroom being used.

I loved working with Elisabeth Bergner on *Dreaming Lips.* I used the technique I used for Marlene in that, with a light over the head. I co-produced it with Paul Czinner. Bergner was a superb actress; Czinner wasn't her equal, but no matter what the direction was, it couldn't hurt her performance. It was like me married to Helen Hayes! You couldn't really do wrong. There was a big problem on the picture: she liked to work at night, she was used to stage hours, and we never seemed to get home. We'd often work from eight a.m. to eight p.m., or other days she wouldn't come in until one p.m. and we'd work until midnight or after. She just couldn't get up, she was a night person.

After that, of course, came *Gone With The Wind*. I was in London working for Korda when I got a cablegram from Selznick asking me to photograph it. You could have knocked me over with a feather because I thought most of the picture had been finished; I'd been reading about it in the Press for months! I got my agent to accept, and I cut my salary almost in half to do it. When I got to Hollywood I realized the picture hadn't been started – except for the Atlanta fire, shot by Ray Rennahan – nor Vivien Leigh set. I did tests of her and she was hired. I worked with George Cukor . . . it wasn't his fault that George was fired. It was David's. He had a very good script, written by Sidney Howard, but David kept fussing around with it. All the preparatory work was based on Sidney Howard's script, but when we started shooting, we were using Selznick's. His own material just didn't play the same.

Cukor was too much of a gentleman to go to Dave and say, 'Look, you silly son-of-a-bitch, your writing isn't as good as Sidney Howard's.' He did the scenes to the best of his ability and they wouldn't play: Cukor still wouldn't tell David that David was at fault. And no one else wanted to tell the Czar he was wrong.

When Cukor left we closed down the picture for a week or so, and Victor Fleming looked at the tests and finished stuff. He didn't give a damn what he said to Selznick, because he was on loan from Metro, so he told him point-blank, 'David, your f – ing script is no f – ing good.' He demanded the Howard script back. He got it back.

I worked for about ten or twelve weeks. We were using a new type of film, with softer tones, softer quality, but David had been accustomed to working with picture-postcard colours. He tried to blame me because the picture was looking too quiet in texture. I liked the look; I thought it was wonderful; and long afterwards he told me he should never have taken me off the picture. I did about a third of the picture; chronologically almost everything up to

Melanie having the baby, except the fire, which was done before I arrived. I prepared the big shot of the dead lying in the railway yard and Scarlett picking her way through, but I didn't shoot it, I was off the picture by then. I never got screen credit.

I went back after that to Korda: for *Lydia*, a remake of *Carnet de Bal* that suffered from bad casting, and for *The Jungle Book*. I loved that. Zoltan Korda was a very fine director for that type of picture. We did the whole jungle thing in Sherwood Lake, Sherwood Forest, not far from here.

I also very much liked doing, for Selznick again, *Since You Went Away*. Stanley Cortez was on the film and he and the director, John Cromwell, didn't get along. Maybe Stanley was taking too much time over the shots, I'm not sure. The art director, William Pereira, built the sets of the house so solid that you couldn't take the walls out. It was so realistic that you had to shoot into some rooms through the windows only. I myself thought this was wrong; why not use a real house anyway? And if you are going to have a studio house, why not be pliable enough to take walls out of the way if you want to? That way you get better lighting and better sound.

Stanley found it very hard to cope with these walls that couldn't be moved because he hadn't had enough experience (he had originally been my operator). Finally, he was called away to war, and went to Russia, and later to do the Yalta Conference, so I came in and finished the film. I did about 50 per cent of it. Like *Gone With The Wind*, it was done chronologically, so that you can take, say, the first half of the running time, and say, Stanley did that. We followed the realism right down to details like making sure that every lamp cast exactly the same beam that it would normally, and that the light always came from precisely the correct source, with nothing cheated at all. It was a film remarkably truthful to life in its visual style.

Guest In The House was a wonderful experience. The sets were made very small, so I used a very wide-angle lens to make them look bigger; the ceilings were made of stretched cheesecloth, and we hung the lights over them. There was one scene in which Aline

MacMahon was in the garden and all there was behind her was a blown-up still photograph of the house; nobody noticed. Lewis Milestone started the picture, and got appendicitis, then André de Toth did it for a couple of weeks and had to leave, and John Brahm finished it.

On *Love Letters* I used the same method I used on *Guest In The House*. I created an artificial landscape: clouds, trees, everything were in the studio. Dieterle, the director, used to go home every night and have dinner, and afterwards he'd have a little tiny set at home which he'd put the actors on in the shape of tiny dried-up peas. He'd move them around to prepare the next day's shooting.

I also did *The Searching Wind* for him, a story about appeasement in Europe between the wars, which wasn't very good. It had a poor cast. And after that I went back to work with Ben Hecht on *Spectre of the Rose*, which was about ballet.

We had one rather interesting shot in that picture. There's a scene in which the male lead ballet dancer dances suicidally out of a window. We rigged up an arm outside a downtown building in Los Angeles and lowered the camera on a cable photographing all the time. Originally we were going to have the shot as a back projection for his fall, as he did his crossing of the feet. Finally, when we got to editing, I suggested reversing the shot; we go up the building, and find he's in there; it gives you a feeling of height, of the long way he's going to fall. It came out very well.

It was very tricky shooting into the long ballet class mirror behind the *barre* without showing the reflection of the camera. I angled the glass slightly, and just got my lights out of the range of vision overhead; the camera was barely out of the frame, but it *was* just out. If I had moved it an inch further, you would have seen it.

I went back to Selznick again for *Duel in the Sun*: he had fired two cameramen – he was up to his old tricks again, and had argued with them over the physical presentation – and I did about 60–70 per cent of the picture. All of the interiors were mine. I did the scene of the galloping of the ranch hands and the clash with the railway when the wires were cut. I did the scene of the meeting of the carriages on the skyline bathed in red on the stage, with every-

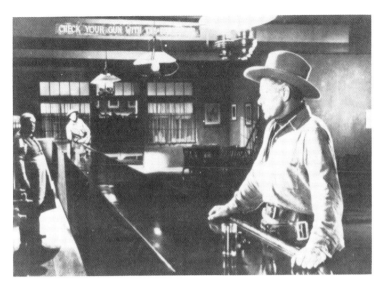

Duel in the Sun: Gregory Peck, Charles Bickford

thing in red gelatins. We were retaking the barbecue picnic scene with the lanterns under the trees on the last day of shooting and just as we got two kids up in the tree watching, we got word that the Japanese had surrendered, and the war was over.

Selznick came out on set and gave us the news. He said, 'Please stay with us and get a good take, and then everyone can go home.' At eleven-thirty we finished, and the picture was over the same day as the war. It was a great moment.

I worked on *Nightmare Alley*, a story about a sideshow man who becomes a famous fake spiritualist in Chicago. I was loaned to do it by Selznick. I had known the director, Edmund Goulding, for many years; he had a brilliant mind. But he was strange; he'd say something that suggested genius, and ten minutes later he'd forget what he had in mind. Luckily he had someone around always to take notes of what he said, and he'd look them up. He was utterly spontaneous. He had no idea of camera; he concentrated on the actors. He liked the camera to follow the actors all the time. He was the only director I've known whose actors never came in out of the sideline of a frame. They either came in a door or down a flight of stairs or from behind a piece of furniture. He liked their entrances and exits to be photographed. I like that; they didn't just 'disappear somewhere' out of the frame-line, as they so often do. But it was 'proscenium-arch' direction: no doubt of it.

I invented – with three others – the crab dolly during the middle of *The Paradine Case*. We made a mock-up of wood; the problem we had to face was that Hitchcock wanted to move into a room, then you'd be able to look back and see all the walls at once. A man called Steve Granovich put it together out of all of our ideas. He later formed a corporation to make and sell them. I should have had a share but didn't. That was my fault, I guess. In the early stages of the film, as the camera is circling round Alida Valli, we had a moveable lamp-stand for the camera. The floor was a little bumpy, but it didn't show. Hitchcock wanted to use four cameras in the trial scene: one on the witness box, one on the judge, one on the prosecuting counsel, one on the defending counsel. I said, 'Sure.' He wanted to do it like the early talkies, like a stage play. Two cameras were on cranes, two were fixed. Later on I did a pilot for Buzz Kulik for *The Defenders* in the same style, and cut out one day of shooting. They used the stage technique through the whole series, with one camera on the box and one on the attorney and simply cutting to and fro, like they used to do way back in 1930.

The late Irving Reis and I had trouble on *Roseanna McCoy*. He was a bastard to work for, even though he was very pleasant off the sound stage. He was a frustrated cameraman who didn't know what he was doing. He wouldn't listen or take advice. On the first day of shooting he was trying to line up a scene and the cutter came in to talk to him. Finally, he turned to all of us and said he didn't want anybody to give him a single idea or suggestion so long as he was on the picture. The cutter got mad and walked off. I didn't, because the only thing I'm concerned about is making a good picture. Reis only took my advice very occasionally. Goldwyn asked me to make the love scenes look very 'soft', as George Barnes used to do for

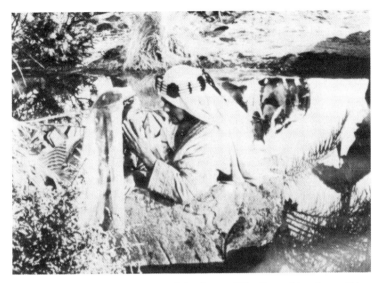

The Big Fisherman: Susan Kohner, John Saxon. 'The finest thing I ever did on the screen . . .'

him. He wanted gauzes. I did what he wanted, and the scenes were very beautiful, but they didn't cut right. The change from hard to soft focus was too abrupt; I should have *slid* into them. Goldwyn kept saying, 'The love scenes are too soft,' after he'd asked for them, too! But he meant the transitions were bad, and he was right.

Detective Story was a raw, harsh picture. I prepared the picture with Willie Wyler; we only had a thirty-six day schedule. I told him if he gave me my head there would be no problem in such a tight schedule. I told him to find a stage with smooth floors at Paramount; if there were any holes in them he must fill them up with putty and sandpaper them. I told him I'd use the crab dolly; he'd never used it before, and he was delighted with the idea of a camera he could move wherever he wanted it. 'Jeez,' he said, 'that will be fantastic.' And I told him to rehearse the actors while I rehearsed the camera and lights at the same time; if I made too

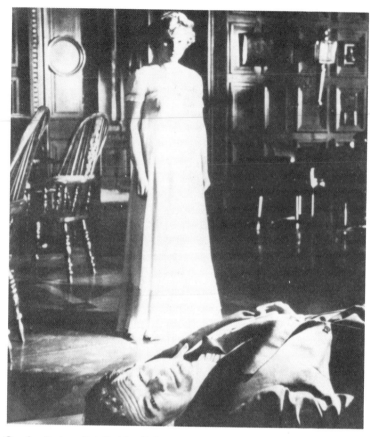

Caught: Barbara Bel Geddes, Robert Ryan

much noise he was to tell me. And then I suggested to him that stills be made of each final rehearsal with the dialogue attached each time, so as to speed up the actual shots. Willie had a ball with the crab dolly! We came in six days under schedule, a record for him.

The Lusty Men, for Nicholas Ray, was a tough job, because we had to do all the outdoor day-time scenes indoors at night! We had run into weather problems and there was no alternative way of handling this story about the people in the rodeos. We had to make

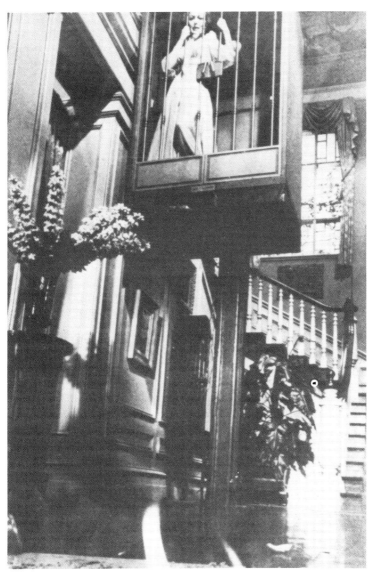

Lady in a Cage: Olivia de Havilland

the scenes bright enough to look like day, without having too many shadows coming from too many improbable directions. We used a white overhead light and for the close-ups I used the north-light effect which gave the illusion they were under the sun. It was all totally artificial, but I don't think anybody knew the difference.

For *Land of the Pharaohs* I returned to work with Howard Hawks, many, many years after *Scarface*. Exteriors were done in Egypt, interiors in Rome. The crab dolly came in very handy going round the narrow corridors of the great pyramids, and there was a superb job done of art direction of the interiors of these by Alexandre Trauner.

I found working with CinemaScope a horror. Shallow focus, very wide angles, everyone lining up: awful. There was no definition at all. The Panavision lenses were far, far superior, and nowadays they have largely replaced CinemaScope. Close-ups used to give fat faces!

The finest thing I ever did on the screen was *The Big Fisherman*. It was very lovely. Everything in that film was magnificent. The best art director in the business, John De Cuir, did the sets. I shot with 1,000-foot candles and stopped the lenses down very hard to get sharp, sharp focus, carried as far as possible. Sometimes we went up to 1,800- or even 2,000-foot candles. The whole film glowed like a series of Rembrandts. I believe that picture will one day be acknowledged to be a visual masterpiece.

In *Lady in a Cage* I had a picture that, like *Guest In The House*, *Since You Went Away*, and *The Desperate Hours*, was all set in one house. It had a good harsh documentary look I'm fond of achieving and a great performance by Olivia de Havilland.

Most recently, I've enjoyed working with Fielder Cook on a couple of pictures: he's the dream boy of all the directors I've worked with. He's very talented. And *very* meticulous. *How to Save a Marriage* was most interesting for me, because it was a comedy treated as a drama in the lighting. In the department-store scenes I had a particular use of light that showed every detail without a single shadow; that's the kind of light they have in stores because they want to have everything seem quite clear to the customers. In the scenes in the young girl's apartment, I had a wholly different kind of lighting, soft and low-key; I varied the lighting according to her mood. She was beautifully played by Stella Stevens, and the camera reflected her changes of feeling. She took the north light very well. We had soft, quiet colours throughout.

At present I'm planning a return to work as a fullscale producer. I have several properties: among them a Western about an Irish girl on her way to Santa Fé as a hospital nun; her wagon-train is massacred; she meets a renegade whom she wants to lead her to her destination. It's a beautiful story. I also want to do *Mission in Teheran*, about the attempted assassination by Nazi agents of Churchill, Roosevelt and Stalin at the Teheran Conference.

I'm very sympathetic with all the cinematic changes that have taken place in Europe in the last ten years or so. We try to be too perfectionist here, and that makes everything look too manufactured. I've always tried to avoid that manufactured, 'Hollywood' look. I've always followed the 'European' look. I was 'New Wave' long before it came along!

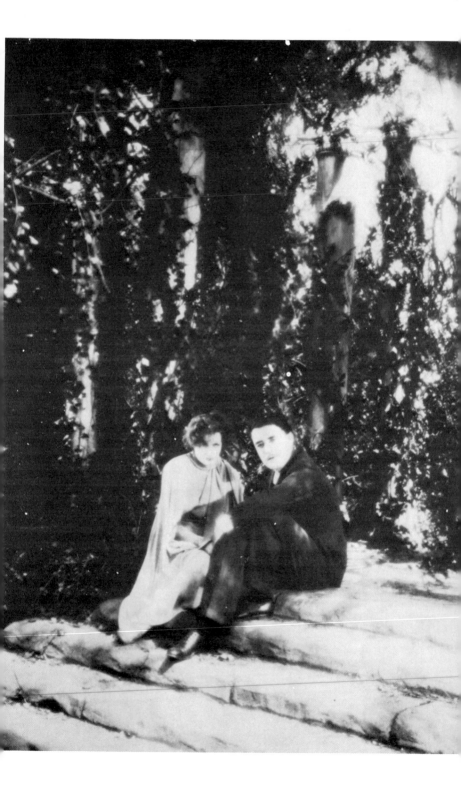

3: William Daniels

Unlike, say, Lee Garmes, I vary my work considerably according to the story. Even my lighting of Garbo varied from picture to picture. There wasn't one Garbo face in the sense that there was a Dietrich face. I'd give each director what he wanted. But of course I could improvise. And the directors always left the lighting to you. For instance, in *Flesh and the Devil* . . . for the arbour love scene I just wanted a faint glow to illuminate Garbo and Gilbert's faces. So I gave Jack Gilbert two tiny little pencil carbons to hold. When they kissed the carbons lit up. His hands shielded the mechanism from the lens.

And then again, I was able to do something interesting in *Mata Hari*. Novarro and Garbo are in a little secluded niche in a restaurant or inn. She is seducing him, and it's very romantic. I wanted to illuminate the whole scene with just the glow from his cigarette alone. I put a special window over their heads so that the smoke would drift up past it and be fully visible. Then I had another idea. I'd been to a doctor and he'd put this tiny tube up my nostrils, with a brilliant little bulb in it. Now I had a dummy cigarette made with one of those medical bulbs in it, and I stuck the ashes on with glue. I mounted another cigarette under it to cause the smoke. I had a little rheostat by the camera and each time he raised the cigarette to his lips I'd bring the bulb up bright. And the smoke would go up. All you'd see was just one gleam. . . .

I think the photographer, the cinematographer, should be an

The Flesh and the Devil: Garbo and Gilbert

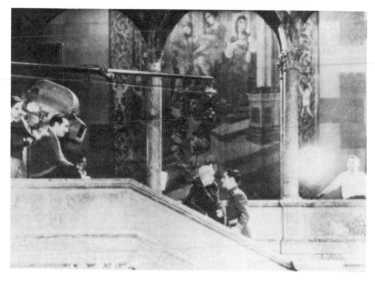

George Fitzmaurice directing Garbo and Novarro in *Mata Hari*; Daniels at camera

inventor of detail, adding to the imagination of a director with his own scientific skills. Beyond that I haven't tried to go. For instance, on *Anna Karenina*: Clarence Brown wanted a striking shot to open the picture, so I went right along a banquet-table, solving the problem by building a special kind of dolly. It had wheels outside the chairs and the camera was suspended over the table. There was room for only me up there. I was on a tiny platform, and we moved eighty or ninety feet over the jugs and dishes.

We came here in my early childhood. I was born in Cleveland; I remember when I was very young seeing a Sennett company working in a park near where we lived. I watched the cameraman closely; he seemed a Very Important Person, if you know what I mean. My mother was fond of cameras; she kept a complete record of all of us on an old Brownie. My father was interested in acting, and was on the stage for a while, but he wasn't too successful, unfortunately. My brother, Jack Daniels, had some success as a stage director and more recently he has been making commercials. He was born in California.

I managed to land a job at the age of fifteen in the old Triangle/KB Studios; they needed an assistant cameraman, and of course I knew nothing about it, but they gave me a job anyway. I got twelve dollars a week. I carried a camera and held a slate . . . we used to do a bit more than the assistants do now, in that regard. We loaded the film magazines and the still camera and carried all of the equipment to the set. My first job as an assistant was on Gloria Swanson's first dramatic film. When the company failed, I went over to Universal, and worked on some of their serials: eighteen episodes of one a week. One of the first ones I worked on was *Robinson Crusoe*. After a year they let me become full photographer, on a one-reel Bert Roach comedy, then I did more comedies and more serials, while working alternately with von Stroheim on his big pictures.

Ben Reynolds was assigned to von Stroheim by the studio and I was assigned as second cameraman. We didn't relish the idea of working with von Stroheim because it was wartime and the German image was a bit of a problem, but we soon got to know him and accepted the idea of being on his team. He was a man well ahead of his time in many technical respects, he was one of the first to insist on no make-up for men, on real paint on walls which were shiny, real glass in windows, pure white on sets and in costumes . . . everything up to then had been painted a dull brown. We learned quite a lot from him. Of course, his big failing was that he just couldn't make a picture within a practical length of time.

At first, his relationship with the studio was a very good one. We worked very hard on *Blind Husbands*, and we made the film within a reasonable length of time. Later on, when he became very ambitious and decided to do *Foolish Wives*, and became used to seeing himself on the screen as an actor, the studio became almost helpless to control him. *Blind Husbands* was a pretty straightforward job for me in that a lot of it was done outside and

59

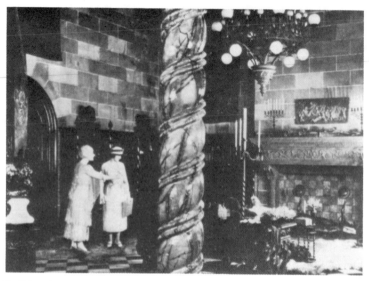

Foolish Wives

the little Tyrolean street we used didn't present too many problems. *The Devil's Passkey* was a more sophisticated story, but I remember nothing more about it than that. Those stories in those days were rather weak, you know. I do remember thinking Maude George in *Passkey* was a fine actress, but cameramen didn't work closely with actresses the way we did later.

Foolish Wives was far more ambitious and interesting. We were on that for some thirteen months. Von Stroheim was terribly, terribly slow; there would be constant rehearsal; he would select 'types', too, for parts, rather than accomplished actors or actresses. It was his job (he was proud of that) to be more or less a Svengali, to turn the 'types' into 'great performers'. That took a terrible lot of time, *endless* time. He was a strange breed that couldn't get started in the morning at all, he couldn't face the light, he was totally a 'night' person. We would never stop for meals at the proper hour. We'd stop for lunch at three and have an evening meal maybe at ten, and then go back to work. We had very little sleep, and no overtime, of course. There were no limits on the hours in those days.

The actors and actresses just didn't complain; it was hell for them, but they were ambitious, and would do anything to succeed. Some he would bully, some not. I remember we had a little girl called Malvine Polo; there was a sequence in which von Stroheim went to her bedroom and there was a rape involved, and she becomes hysterical. We worked all night long on that one scene. She wasn't an accomplished actress, and finally he worked her so hard that she actually became hysterical. That was when he got what he wanted. It was his technique, you might say, to get novices and drive them to the point at which they lived a part, since they couldn't 'act' it. Extraordinary, but far too costly, and not practical in any sense of the word.

We shot the scenes of the Riviera château at Point Loomis, Monterey. It was built right on a cliff. The whole Promenade at Monte Carlo was built there, too; storms played havoc with our set and destroyed a good portion of it; that only added to a host of problems.

As to directing his own performance, von Stroheim always had an assistant to give him an opinion of his acting; whether he listened to it or not was another matter! We did a scene at Lake Forest in which the boats were reflected in von Stroheim's monocle; we were down there several nights when the studio decided finally he had had enough time. When I went to the location next night the cameras weren't there. I got a car and went after the cameras, but I couldn't get them back. Thalberg had removed them permanently. By the time I got back they had taken the lights away. Thalberg was terrified, and I sympathize; spending all that time, and a million dollars, on a picture in those days was incredible, unheard of.

What also added to the expense was the extraordinary realism of the Monterey 'Monte Carlo', a streetcar, a casino to scale, a hotel, a huge plaza, and to light this vast creation we had to rent lights from many other studios, because we had exhausted the whole of Universal's supply. Just lighting alone for months on end cost fortunes and fortunes.

You remember there was a scene on a tower which catches fire: a girl sets fire to it and commits suicide by jumping into the sea. We had a very big set on the backlot, and used doubles of course, up in the tower, and the prop shop men arranged the fire, with the aid of torches and some inflammable material, gasoline, I guess. There was a near disaster there: we put the camera across the street from the entrance to the huge place. The scene called for the firemen to drive up to the area and line up for inspection, and then run into the building. All this took time, and von Stroheim insisted on absolute accuracy; in the meantime the flames were rising and rising, and the doubles were still up there on the balcony, we heard cries, and by the time the firemen had the net ready, the net the stand-ins could jump into, they were singed very, very badly.

I experimented with some halo-like effects round hair in that picture. I used a thin net like a lady's stocking over the lens. The effect was of a sort of vignette. You could burn it out with a cigarette into different shapes. There was one scene in which we had a monk in a cabin by candlelight; the candlelight made a little crosslight, and von Stroheim liked that.

As I said, the film took thirteen months to shoot. They did the advance publicity and they started to edit it. It took months to do that. He wanted to make it a huge film, shown over three nights, and let it run in its final cut 125 reels! The studio, of course, couldn't accept that concept at all. They were falling behind for the New York première, so they outfitted a baggage car and took the whole film in the car and had an editor cutting it down on the train, the train to New York. They at last got it to New York for the opening at a reasonable length.

Von Stroheim's next picture, *Merry-Go-Round*, was a disaster for him. He wasn't playing a part in that film, so he didn't have the power he had had before; if he *had* played a part, they would have hesitated to take him out of it, because so much of the valuable film would have been lost. In the big banquet scene he had all the extras playing Austrian officers *really* drunk; he served real champagne by the bucketful and whisky as well; all the extras got loaded. A girl stepped naked out of a punchbowl . . . stuff like that. I think it was during a shot when I irised in on her that von Stroheim passed out cold! He went further and further behind schedule, and spent far too much time and money, and I think the studio of necessity had to do something about it. He was taken away from the picture quietly, and Rupert Julian was put in. Julian was one of the mediocre directors of that time.

Von Stroheim came back for *Greed*; we were seven months on that. Much of it was very hard going. We were six weeks in Death Valley during the summer – July and August. It was 132 degrees under the shade of an umbrella. Of course, being a realist he really *had* to have it hot! Luckily it was dry heat, and we were all young, and could stand it. The only water was at Furnace Creek Ranch, which the English Borage Company kept supposedly for agricultural purposes. There was a lake with palm trees and we lived on little army cots in the open air. It was too hot for tents. I remember the beautiful stars through the palm trees at night. The food was horrible. We had a camp cook. And ice was a problem: it had to be brought down in burlap bags in a case covered with sawdust. The trucks weren't much good in those days. The cast stood up well except for Jean Hersholt, who became hysterical at one stage with the bad sunburn. At that time Death Valley was considered truly to be Death Valley; so many men had lost their lives there. The mountains on each side are so high and the distance so great that you lose all perspective: you look across the valley and you think you can walk it easily, but actually it's twenty-five to thirty-five miles to the foothills.

We used natural interiors in the scenes in San Francisco. It was one of the first times they had been used. The company rented one whole building. We had a big scene they still talk about: the wedding of McTeague and the girl, and during the wedding procession you see a funeral cortège going by, through the window. In other scenes you see the streetcar passing. It was done without process. There was a problem of getting a correct balance of light between

The Merry Widow: John Gilbert, Mae Murray→

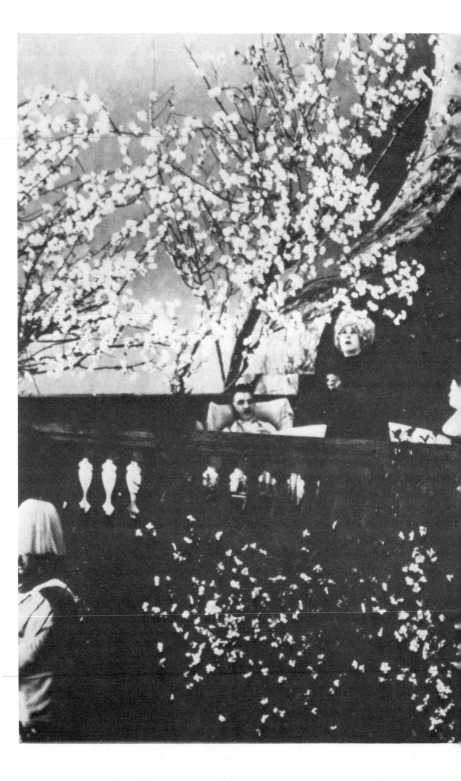

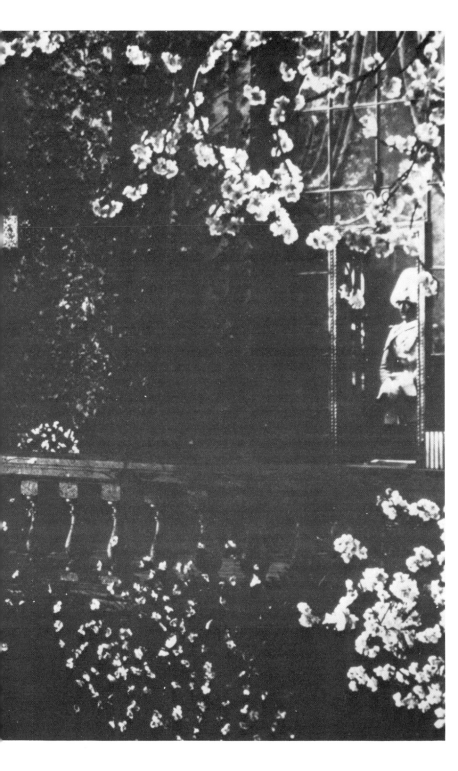

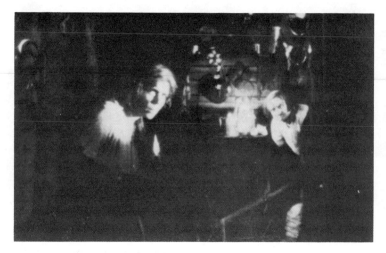

Greed: Dale Fuller and Cesare Gravina. 'We spent months lighting their shack . . .'

interior and exterior so that it looked as though all the scenes were lit by daylight only, and getting enough light on the people to balance the exposure was hell.

We used for the very first time some incandescent lights for that film. A problem with the arcs was that they would smoke, and that made it all very hard. Realism got us into trouble in the gold-mining scenes at the start. Von Stroheim insisted we went into the mine to a depth of 3,000 feet – it was at Colefax, Northern California, I remember – instead of at 100 feet, which would have got us exactly the same effects!

Of course, so much of my best work was cut from the picture. Originally it had a lot about a junk-man and his wife, and they were completely – no, *almost* completely – taken out. We spent months lighting their shack so carefully, to make it real, and it was all wasted. Months, for instance, colouring each *candle flame* with a one-hair brush! On every print! It was shown that way in New York, I guess, but never again. It wasn't too successful, anyway, and you can imagine the way we felt after all those months with

magnifying glasses colouring the flames, day after day after day.
. . . And all the flames did was jiggle . . .

The Merry Widow involved the same hectic, twenty-hour
schedules as before. We had to bring in two crews: electricians and
everyone. There were constant battles between Mae Murray and
von Stroheim; she wanted the full star treatment, and he refused
to give that to her; he disliked the whole idea of stars. He tried to
treat her as an ordinary person, and make her give a realistic
performance, and she hated that.

The Merry Widow ended my association with von Stroheim.
Soon after that, I began to work with Garbo. My memory of my
first meeting with her is very clear. We were working very, very
hard, I recall, and it was quite common to come in Sunday. They
asked me to come in one Sunday morning and do some tests of a
Swedish girl. She had just arrived. I didn't like that idea at all. I
didn't like working Sunday too well. But I came in, of course.
I made a few simple close-ups of her. She couldn't speak one word
of English and was terrifically shy. She didn't enjoy it any better
than I did. It was an ordeal for both of us. But they just had to
have the record of what she could do.

There she was, in the midst of a strange people and a strange
language, and it must have been a horrifying experience for her.
The close-ups I had to do very carefully, because of course we
don't have the benefit of retouching that the portrait studio has.
We lit very much to find their best features and accent those
features strongly. Especially eyes. And Garbo had magnificent
eyes. She looked much better photographed from the left and I
always insisted that directors took note of that. It wasn't a real
problem, though, with her as it was with many stars: you *could*
use both sides if you had to.

I was the one who insisted on the closed sets for her. No visitors,
and so on, no one present except the director and the crew, and no
executives. I was trying to help her, especially because it took her
a time to speak English, and she was so shy, *so* shy. I did it to
protect her. And then, she had never been on stage, so she wasn't
accustomed to acting in front of an audience, and she was, quite

Faces of Garbo: (*left column*) *The Torrent, Mata Hari, Susan Lenox, Her Fall
and Rise;* (*centre*) *Anna Karenina, The Kiss, The Flesh and the Devil;* (*right*)
Anna Christie, As You Desire Me→

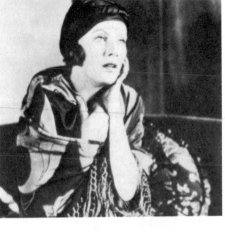
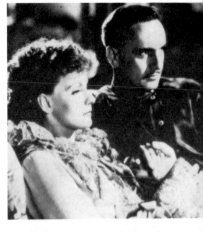
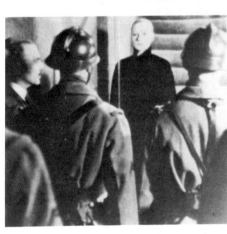
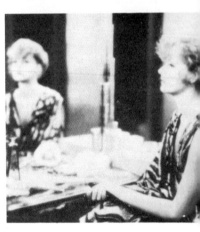
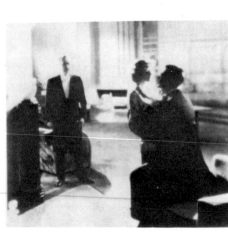
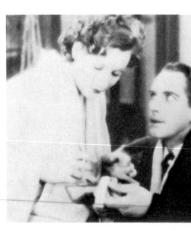

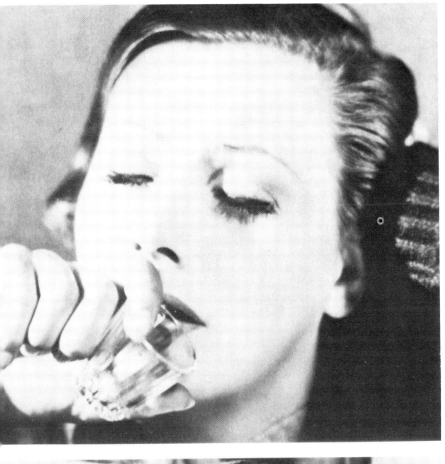

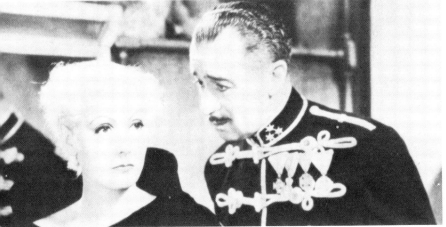

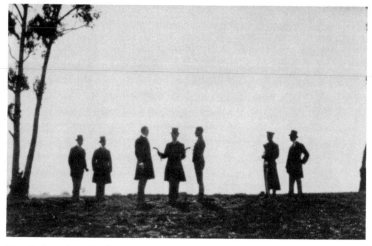

The Flesh and the Devil

simply, suffering constantly from stage fright. I don't know how any actor stands acting in front of set visitors, unless they have had their training in the theatre, when they probably enjoy it. A bunch of staring, gum-chewing people! Whispering away . . . this acting for the screen is very enclosed, very serious.

I didn't create a 'Garbo face'. I just did portraits of her I would have done for any star. My lighting of her was determined by the requirements of a scene. I didn't, as some say I did, keep one side of the face light and the other dark. But I did always try to make the camera peer into the eyes, to see what was there. Garbo had natural long eyelashes and in certain moods I could throw the light down from quite high, and show the shadows of the eyelashes come down on the cheeks: it became a sort of trade mark with her. Her eyelashes were real; after I did that many stars got false ones and had their cameramen do the same lighting for them, but it wasn't quite the same thing.

Of course, you didn't always want a feeling of 'mystery'; on *Ninotchka*, you wanted just the *opposite* effect. I remember we would devise various interesting things in scenes with her: that still illustrating my work in an article in *Sight and Sound*, showing her and John Gilbert in a grove, shimmered because it was shot through gauze.

Flesh and the Devil also had a scene of pistol duellists in silhouette. Clarence Brown had the idea for that; he drove along La Cienega Boulevard to work each morning and he would notice these stark trees in silhouette against the white buildings. We had to build a platform for the camera way, way back from the scene: it was almost like building a bridge. The difficulty was to maintain a proper level to ensure the silhouette worked. I always admire this thoroughness in Brown. He's a great technician and a fine director. I see him quite often now.

The Kiss was the first film of Lew Ayres. Jacques Feyder couldn't speak English so we engaged a German who interpreted for the rest of us while Garbo and Feyder talked in German. It got to be quite complicated and it wasn't necessary anyway because I spoke some French!

Then we got into the sound period, and the cameras in those butchers' iceboxes. And very few people knew anything about editing sound: there is a scene at the beginning of *Anna Christie* they often refer to in which the camera travels a long, long way across a wharf, and we had mist and water lapping. Well, the reason for long scenes like that was that they just weren't sure how to sound edit! On *The Trial of Mary Dugan*, for instance, they used six cameras: they had no way of editing the track so they just took a single sound-track for every single angle. Everything came out at the same volume. They'd cut a wax disc and when they'd finished we'd go in and run 800 or 900 feet of film in one go.

On *As You Desire Me*, I again worked with von Stroheim, but this time as an actor; George Fitzmaurice was directing. Von Stroheim came up to me at a quarter of six one evening and said, 'It's time to quit, isn't it?' He wanted to go home . . . he was an actor now!

One of my biggest challenges of the thirties was *Rasputin and the Empress*. We all spent a great deal of time on research for this film. I ran a lot of stock film made in Russia in Rasputin's time, but unfortunately it was unusable because the grain in it was so bad; so I had to reconstruct the time *as though it were* a newsreel. I had to aim for harshness, nothing glossy, we used sunlight exactly as it is, without the slightest addition of reflected light. If we saw a face it was with the natural shadows; that was unusual in Hollywood at that time.

We were lucky in that at that time. In the black and white era, which is now over, we had absolute control over the images by way of a fine film laboratory. By certain tricks we could do things like under-expose the film and have it overdeveloped to increase the contrast, and vice versa, to soften the contrast. In this film, we worked very hard to achieve an unusually stark series of contrasts . . . I won't say we wanted 'newsreel realism' ('newsreel' is a dirty word in our vocabulary photographically speaking), but it was real.

I suppose the most notable moment in *Queen Christina* was when Garbo strokes the bedroom. All the light in the room came from the fire – or seemed to; of course we had to cheat a little by using special small spotlights that illuminated the bedposts, the furniture, in such a way that they seemed to be the kind of light flickering flames would make. A problem was that the scene had to be done in a very subdued, natural light and still be practical for theatre display. I think I learned the realism in this scene, the way of achieving it, from von Stroheim.

Reflection was a very valuable tool, I liked reflections. Many of the cameramen used to spray everything with oil to make it shiny, to avoid reflections, they thought they were a nuisance. Television today has to avoid reflections, because you get light flares on the screen if you shoot into a mirroring surface, and you get a black image as a result. I was determined to have reflections because of what von Stroheim had taught me, and I had them, though they did create difficulties. You see, *we try to tell the story with light as the director tries to tell it with his action.*

When Garbo and Norma Shearer left Metro, I sat around for years doing little things because there wasn't much going on.

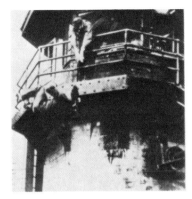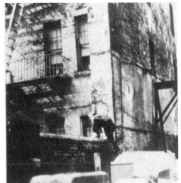

Brute Force and *The Naked City:* post-war realism

Finally, I left Metro – I was ill for some time – and joined Universal. *The Naked City*, which I did there, was shot in actual apartments; I think we only used one set. We developed some small unit lights to meet the problem. We used a very fast film and overexposed it slightly to bring the extreme contrast of the outside and the dimmer light inside together without any obvious difference of time. The lab men worked very closely with us. You can't do that now; our laboratory work today is done by time, and there isn't any time for fiddling around, for improving.

I suppose of all the films that I've done in recent years the one I'm most proud of is *Plymouth Adventure*, which reunited me with Clarence Brown. We had the whole ship hinged at one end. The camera was suspended on a long boom. We wanted to show the people leaning. It was hard to light: we had little tiny units . . . it was so crowded there with beams and everything; the moment you moved your set the lights would be seen. We kept the camera moving constantly. The special effects of the storm were the best I've photographed.

I enjoyed working with Anthony Mann. He was a good director and a fine man. Of the films made with him, I liked *Strategic Air Command* the best, and *The Glenn Miller Story*. In *Strategic Air*

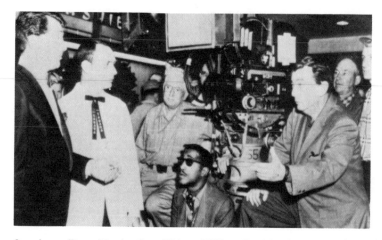

Ocean's 11: Dean Martin, Joey Bishop, William Daniels, Sammy Davis Jnr, Lewis Milestone

Command, after months of tests and searches, I decided to use a B-36 and fly in it directly over the huge glass nose, shooting through the Plexiglass bubble. We flew at sunset and shot the crosslight. And we'd use the vapour trail because if you shoot a plane against a blue sky with nothing else in the shot it doesn't seem to be moving. The effects of the coloured clouds were very beautiful, and nothing was faked.

On *The Glenn Miller Story* I really got a chance to do something new. Or something that in a different form was what Disney had experimented with in his films. That was the last of the three-colour films, and I wanted to do something interesting. So in the scene of the jazz session in the cellar with Louis Armstrong I measured the light waves against the sound-waves from each instrument and matched them, so that as far as I could I had each instrument coloured by the lights according to the equal frequency of the sound, red for one instrument, blue for another and so on. These are the kinds of pleasures a cameraman rarely gets. And when they come, they make the whole thing worthwhile.

4: James Wong Howe

I have a basic approach that goes on from film to film: to make all the sources of light absolutely naturalistic. If you are in a room and the scene is taking place at a certain time of day, try to find out where the light would come from, and follow that, don't impose an artificial style. In colour that's difficult to control, and I prefer black and white, but we have no more black and white in Hollywood. You can fake a 'true' look in the colour laboratory but then it becomes an achievement of chemistry, not of cinematography.

I've had problems with fakery in films: in *The Thin Man*, the director wanted shadows because it was a mystery, too many shadows. Often I didn't see where a light was in a room to make a shadow, but he'd say, 'There's a blank space on the wall, let's fill it,' and I'd make him a shadow. I threw away naturalism on that picture, unfortunately. I would have liked to use locations on *Kings Row*, and on *Seconds* I didn't want the wide-angle lens, the bug-eye. I wanted that journey to the operating-theatre to be done in a simple style, with subjective camera. But John Frankenheimer differed.

Occasionally you can do inventive things with colour. I remember on my very first Technicolor feature, *The Adventures of Tom Sawyer*. The cave scene when the children are lost after the picnic was superbly designed by William Cameron Menzies. It was hard to do; Technicolor in those days called for the use of 800–1,000

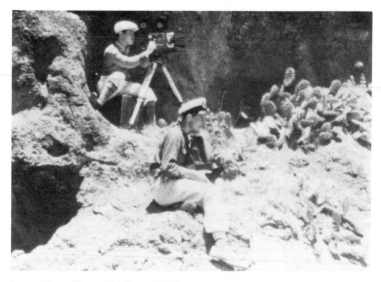

James Wong Howe with Ronald Colman, c. 1929

foot candles. And if I'd used them the cave would have been over-lit. So Selznick agreed to let me use 350-foot candles – I wanted them shorter still, but I had to compromise a little. You see, the labs kept saying, we can't do good prints, we'll have to continue making new matrices, the prints will be too dark. So I said, make new matrices then. Luckily, Selznick gave me freedom. Now all the light in that great cave had to come from Tom Sawyer's candle. The screen had to be black until the kids came in and then all you saw was the flickering glow and the darkness had to close in behind them.

It was impossibly difficult in colour. We tried hiding lights and dimming them, but it didn't work. So I got some pince-nez for the kids to wear, to protect their eyes, and I built a harness and put a globe in front of the boy so that it threw the light up through an imitation candle. I had a little shade so it didn't overlight his hands and a kind of diffuser at the back so it would look as though the light was coming entirely from the candle. If the dripping water Selznick wanted for realism had hit the globe, the globe would have blown up and injured the boy. But the effect was what I wanted, and I love to create fully in this way. Luckily, most directors leave the lighting to me.

I came over to America from China when I was five; that was in 1904. I was born in Canton. My father, who was a storekeeper, used to wear a cue, like an Indian, his hair braided in one long plait: and that was what they used to wear in the mines in those days. We settled in a town called Pasco, Washington, where the Northern Pacific railroad ran through; one of the boys I knew in those days was Bing Crosby.

Around twelve or thirteen years of age, I bought a little box camera, a Brownie, in a drugstore, and I took pictures of my brothers and sisters. My father was an old-fashioned Chinese; they are superstitious about having their pictures taken, but I went ahead and took head shots, body shots of the whole family. Several years passed, and my father died; in 1914 I went and lived with an Irish family, in Oregon, and three years later moved in with my uncle. I trained as a boxer and fought around a while. Then I moved to San Francisco after that to join an aviation school; I became a delivery boy in Los Angeles for a commercial photographer. One night I helped a friend who was going back to China by doing some passport photos in the firm's laboratory, and I was dismissed.

A job as bus boy at the Beverly Hills Hotel followed. On Sunday I'd go to Chinatown and watch a comedy being shot; I spoke to the cameraman – I noted he wore his cap backwards in keeping with the tradition – and he suggested I should come into movies. If I went to a studio, I could ask for an assistant's job. A few months later I dropped in to the Jesse Lasky Studios on Ninth Street (Famous Players) and the man in charge of photography told me I was too small and frail to carry equipment. Instead he hired me to pick up scraps of nitrate stock from the cutting-room floor.

The salary was ten dollars a week. I took the job. I graduated to slate boy for Mr De Mille. He told Alvin Wyckoff to keep me on as a third assistant; I worked for the Japanese cameraman Henry Kotani, who was specializing in Sessue Hayakawa pictures. I helped with a picture called *Puppy Love*, co-starring Lila Lee; I did things for Bert Glennon – a picture called *Ebb Tide*, shot at Catalina. I remember we had a scene of rain; the director said to me: 'What did you think of that?' I told him we wouldn't see anything on the screen except a white effect like a sheet; there was so much light back of the rain that everything was blotted out. I said it wasn't my place to point it out or I would have, unasked. It was Mr Glennon's responsibility.

Soon after we had orders to retake the rain scenes, and I was 'in', I was the white-haired boy, and was to report if I saw anything going wrong. In another picture soon after that I got my chance: Bert Glennon took sick, and I did shots for a couple of days. They liked the close-ups at the studio; I had been experimenting with portraiture on the side. I made Dorothy Dalton, the star of the picture, look unusually beautiful, I think. The shots were done in the old glass studios, with black or white cloth on the glass according to whether it was day or night, and that would diffuse the daylight appropriately. It was quite crude and simple, really. Most of the photography was flat, no shadows, and Mr De Mille, who set the tone of so much of Hollywood, insisted you should be able to see everything with equal clarity.

Soon after the Dalton film I was doing some further close-ups and a movie star called Mary Miles Minter walked by (we are talking about 1922 at this stage). Mr De Mille let me make some stills of her; she liked them; she asked me, in fact, to be her personal cameraman. What attracted her in my work was that I made her eyes dark. They were in fact a pale blue; orthochromatic film lightened them too much and made them expressionless. I wondered what made the eyes dark, and I suddenly realized that the darkness was caused by the reflection of light off black velvet which happened to be lying in the little stills-room.

So I had a big frame of black velvet made and a hole cut in the centre; putting the lens through, I did all her close-ups that way.

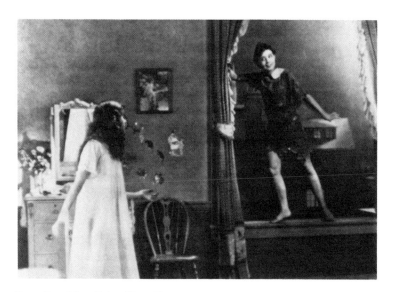

Peter Pan: Mary Brian, Betty Bronson

I raised the incandescent lights a little to cast shadows on the face; she was happy with the effects I caused. Word got around that Mary Miles Minter had found herself a new Chinese cameraman: they thought I had been specially imported! The black velvet was something new. Soon everyone with blue eyes wanted me to photograph them, and I was launched.

One of my first pictures with Miss Minter was *Drums of Fate*; later I made *The Trail of the Lonesome Pine* for her. Herbert Brenon called me in to do *The Spanish Dancer*, with Pola Negri and Adolphe Menjou: it had big, big settings, out on the Lasky Ranch, a huge castle where Forest Lawn is now; we had 3,000 extras. Oddly enough, Mary Pickford was doing a film at the same time with exactly the same theme: *Rosita*. Mr Brenon liked me, so we went on working together; and on *Peter Pan*, with Betty Bronson, I suppose you could say I had my first big chance to be imaginative.

This chance came with the treatment of the little fairy figure of Tinkerbell. Mr Brenon told me that when Maude Adams played Peter Pan on the stage they used a mirror which made the reflected light dance about. I told Mr Brenon that the light would have to hit a surface, it could not be seen on screen if it was just in mid-air. I suggested having a little automobile headlight bulb put on the finest wire the electricians could manage and hung on a fishing-pole, with some Christmas tinsel on the bulb like a tiny skirt. Then the bulb could be moved up and around. He said: 'The mirror light was good enough for Maude Adams; it's good enough for us.'

I did some tests of both; we finally used my idea. I even had a dimmer in the tiny bulb so it could go off and on as I dictated; you even felt Tinkerbell was *breathing*. When the fairy died the light just went out on cue; it was wonderful.

I remember *The Woman With Four Faces* well. Richard Dix was in gaol at San Quentin and Betty Compson, his girl, arrived disguised as his mother; she told him help would come from above, and it did, literally, because while the prisoners were playing baseball in the yard a plane flew in with a ladder, he grabbed it, and climbed it. I mounted the camera on the plane and we flew down, zoomed in, sideslipped and so on into the prison. I noticed after the second or third shot there was a guy who kept pointing a rifle at us and firing! It wasn't a gag, it was a guard! We had gotten to the prison before the official permission arrived for us to shoot. It came by car, while we flew. So the prison people thought ours was an escape plan for real.

I remember one night I was leaving the studio quite late and I saw a figure in glasses with a shawl, obviously an old, old woman, maybe a janitress. Suddenly I realized it wasn't a woman when a man's voice came out and spoke some lines from Betty Compson's prison visit. Herbert Brenon, the director, was rehearsing for realism! He was using himself! In the mother role! He used to do that with every part before the next day's shooting. I saw him three years before he died, in his little bungalow on Lexington Avenue, and we talked about the early days; his mind was still bright and clear. He was left out of the business; it wasn't

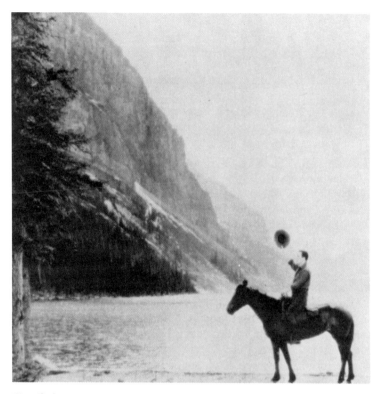

The Alaskan

right. In this business you live on your last picture. It's terribly insecure.

In the mid twenties somewhere I made *The Alaskan*, also for Brenon, with Estelle Taylor and Thomas Meighan. It was about the Royal Canadian Mounted Police. With orthochromatic film I had done the interiors quite well. When I came to that wonderful landscape, with snow-capped mountains and great cloudscapes, I decided to use panchromatic, using a filter. The blue sky would go dark and the clouds would emerge brightly and the mountains would shine with intense brilliance in the light. In orthochromatic the blue would go white. Well, we shot the stuff, and there was supposed to be a scene when the mounties come out of a cabin and suddenly they are in Canada. The cabin scene was done back in Hollywood. We sent back the dailies and a wire arrived: 'Why did you change the mounties' coats?' The jackets had come out white because when I put the red filter in to make the blue sky dark it also made the red go white! To this day I never revealed what went wrong; I just put the orthochromatic film back in quietly, and went on. The skies came out white, but that was too bad.

I also got out of a jam on Brenon's *Side Show of Life*. It was supposed to be a summer story of a circus but we shot it in winter on Long Island. One day so much snow came down that the tent collapsed and we barely got out before it caved in. I enjoyed working with Victor Fleming on *Mantrap*, with Clara Bow. He had lots of good ideas; for instance when Clara Bow is in her attorney's office crying he had me open up on her little hand-mirror showing the lips being made up and I would dolly back and it's Miss Bow for the first time. It was a complicated dolly shot; like everything else in the cinema, dollies like that came out about that time; there hasn't been much improvement or added technique since. I used to think I was the first to use hand-held camera in a feature in *Body and Soul*, but Sidney Franklin made use of it quite often.

The Rough Riders, also for Fleming, introduced a crude version of the crab dolly. He asked me to figure something out to follow the action. I figured out with a camera department man called Madigan a device like a cart on aeroplane wheels and a two-armed thing with a counterbalance and a camera on each arm. You could lift them up or drop them down as you pulled the cart along to follow the action. It worked well. There was an article on it later in *Popular Mechanics*.

I always remember the sight of 400 buckjumpers trying out their skill in breaking in horses for our tests at San Antonio; there was so much dust you couldn't see anything except vague figures flying dismounted through the air. Teddy Roosevelt had made the sport popular and everyone wanted to be in the picture. Bill Wellman was making *Wings* there at the time.

Sorrell and Son took me to England for the first time. We shot it near Maidenhead, with Nils Asther, Mary Nolan and H. B. Warner. It was straightforward. For *Laugh, Clown, Laugh* I used a flat light when Lon Chaney was young and a crosslight when he was old. He was amazing: he had the make-up for his younger days *over* the onion skin that showed the wrinkles and lines of age, and his own skin was under that.

I remember when we were making *Four Walls*, with Joan Crawford. She was so quiet and domestic, she was sitting chewing gum all the time before takes and making the kitchen curtains for her new home with Doug Fairbanks. The director used to come along and say, 'Come on Joan, park your gum under the seat and put down the curtains and play the scene.' She'd get up and go right through a very dramatic scene, crying and everything, then she'd go back and unwrap some more gum and pick up the curtains.

When sound came in I was in China shooting backgrounds for a movie I planned to direct myself, a kind of documentary about the farmers. A lot of the stuff was later used in *Shanghai Express*, and matched in with Lee Garmes's work. I got back, and couldn't get a job; they asked me if I'd made a sound picture and I had to say I'd been away. They told me the new movies were altogether different and they had no place for me.

After a year out of work I met William K. Howard, a very talented director, by chance. I told him I was looking for a job, and I went to see him at Fox. He was also in the doghouse; he had had some run-ins with the front office. He showed me some tests that he had done; the cameraman hadn't corrected the lens properly for the incandescent lights they had switched to by then in Hollywood, and the scenes came out of focus. I bought some lenses for 700 dollars – the price of one lens today – and did some new tests. He let me take a week over them so I could pay my rent. They liked the tests, and I went ahead.

Well, the picture, *Transatlantic*, was something remarkable. I

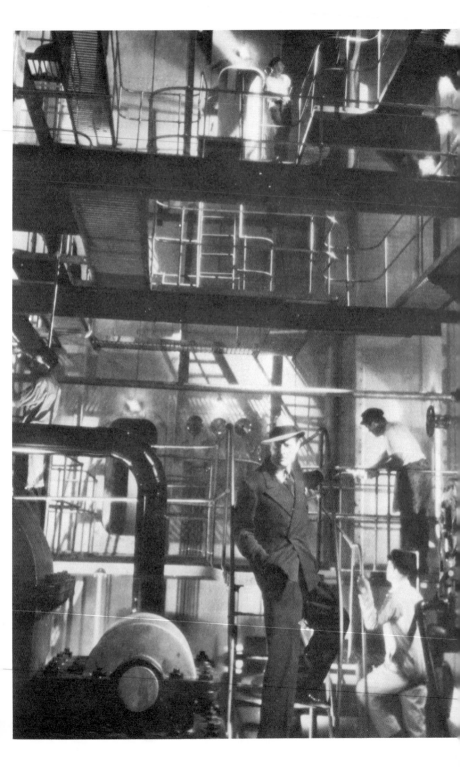

used wide angles, deep focus throughout, long before *Kane*. Eighty per cent of the picture was shot with a twenty-five millimetre lens. The picture was about a travelling con man on the transatlantic run, with Edmund Lowe, Myrna Loy and Jean Hersholt.

I carried focus from five feet back to twenty, thirty feet. I argued with the art director, Gordon Wiles: I wanted ceilings to give the claustrophobic feeling of a ship. He did full ceilings and half ceilings for me, and I used special lights in the engine-room to give an illusion of depth, with special sets of machinery one behind the other. Wiles had built the sets for a fifty-millimetre, two-inch lens, and I told them they were too big. Mr Howard and I made him change everything and there were constant quarrels, but after the picture was released Wiles was perfectly happy: he won the Oscar for set design.

I remember after *Transatlantic* people pointed out that the camera had started to move in the talkies.

The Criminal Code was my first picture with Howard Hawks. I shot about 80 per cent of the picture and I was taken off; to this day I don't know why. They put Ted Tetzlaff on. What may have happened was that Tetzlaff was under contract and had finished another picture and they had to use him; I was just hired for the one picture. There were some quite effective things there, in the prison, in an office scene, it had quite a strong photographic quality. At that time I worked mainly in low key; they called me 'Low-Key Howe'.

I did *The Yellow Ticket* with Laurence Olivier. Raoul Walsh directed him very roughly – Olivier was a beginner, and he was very uncomfortable. *Chandu The Magician* was much more rewarding, co-directed by William Cameron Menzies and Marcel Varnel, with most unusual lighting. But of that period the most remarkable picture I worked on was *Hello, Sister*, or as it was before, *Walking Down Broadway*, with von Stroheim at the helm.

People were frightened of him, he was so dictatorial, so obsessed with detail. I was scared when I was assigned to the picture. But we got along fine, we had respect for each other. I remember many things from his version.

85

Transatlantic: Edmund Lowe. '. . . illusion of depth'

We had a dime-a-dance hall in it. He said, 'Jimmy, I want a dancing camera.' I told him I didn't know what he meant. He said, 'A camera I can move around the floor with, like a dancer.' I was baffled. Finally he grabbed hold of a light-stand and said that we could set a camera on it. I told him it wouldn't stay on, it was too heavy, so I had a heavier lampstand made up. The effect was wonderful.

ZaSu Pitts was burnt in a fire and she lay under a canopy in a hospital. We put electric light bulbs under it and it created a great effect. It was medically accurate – they need a certain temperature I believe – and it was pictorially beautiful. There were lanterns in the streets; von Stroheim wanted them hand tinted. Then when the fire department came in he wanted the fire department lights to be red but everything else black and white. They wouldn't let him do it, and then after it was finished Raoul Walsh came in and reshot a lot of it.

I went out to see von Stroheim after this disaster at his huge house in Beverly Hills. I rang the bell, he came in the door and showed me into this huge living-room. It was completely empty except for one couch in front of the fireplace. 'Jimmy,' he told me, 'they've taken everything. I sleep here on this couch. I don't even have wood to burn in the fire. I use newspapers on my body to keep warm.' He had spent all his money, he had none left. About four reels of the picture are still his. I finished it with Walsh.

The Power and The Glory, done for William K. Howard, was a precursor of *Citizen Kane*. It was about a man whose life is recalled through the eyes of several people; Preston Sturges wrote the script. We began with a funeral, and a tycoon's friends relate how he grew up and worked on the railroad and met a school-teacher whom he fell in love with; she taught him; and then married him. But she committed suicide when he had an affair with another woman. She walked into a car. You see everything through the different eyes of the characters as the thing is pieced together. In London, Howard ran the picture for René Clair and he was deeply impressed. That was when we did *Fire Over England*.

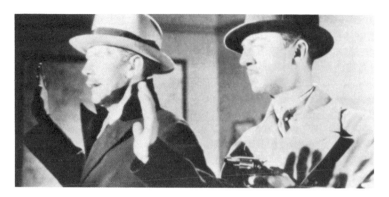

The Thin Man: William Powell with gun

W. S. Van Dyke was a very fast director of those days. We made *Thin Man* in eighteen days and *Manhattan Melodrama* in twenty-eight. He'd come on at nine and the cameras would be turning; at twelve we'd break for lunch, back at one, then leave at five. The first picture was finished, we took three days off, then we did *Melodrama.* That was the way we worked then. In *Thin Man* Van Dyke wanted a lot of shadows, too many I thought. I wanted it stripped of shadows, except for one effect when the thin man, the detective Nick Charles, walks and casts a long, long thin shadow. All the shadows he wanted would dissipate the effect. We disagreed, and finally we compromised.

Tod Browning, for whom I made *Mark of the Vampire*, was quite a character. He had just made *Freaks*. We tested Rita Hayworth as a vampire. He was one of the old school who didn't know much about the camera. He had the actors play 'at' the camera instead of moving around it, so the picture was very stagy, and he used cutting to get him through. We had cobwebs and a low fog on a graveyard achieved before fog machines with dry ice, that kind of thing. Bela Lugosi was funny; he lived the part of the vampire.

Fire Over England for William K. Howard was a huge picture, in England. English crews were slower than American, and I had to get used to the tempo. But those tea-breaks with Queen Elizabeth and her Court were wonderful! I'm afraid Howard's drinking wrecked his career after that picture.

I deeply admired John Cromwell, for whom I made *Prisoner of Zenda*. Selznick, who produced it, liked me, and I had done some tests of Dietrich for *The Garden of Allah*, which I would have done if I hadn't been committed to *Fire*. I remember Dietrich had a full-length mirror alongside her at all times to judge the light. She would tell me what she wanted.

The Prisoner of Zenda had to be rather rich and glistening because of its splendid settings. By contrast, *Abe Lincoln in Illinois*, which I made around the outbreak of war, was much plainer, based partly on Matthew Brady. I experimented there: I lit faces by torchlight only, simply implementing them with reflectors. I made very soft shadows and insisted on bare sets.

Yankee Doodle Dandy, the George M. Cohan musical, had very few photographic opportunities; I had to create them. Mike Curtiz knew almost nothing about lighting; he couldn't even tell the cameraman how he wanted the lights to look. He was very dominating, and many of his ideas wouldn't work. The dances were done by Busby Berkeley, and I enjoyed doing those more, but generally it was an uninteresting picture cinematically.

Kings Row I loved doing. William Cameron Menzies designed the sets and did the sketches for the shots; he'd tell you how high the camera should be. He'd even specify the kind of lens he wanted for a particular shot; the set was designed for one specific shot only, and if you varied your angle by an inch you'd shoot over the top. Everything, even the apple orchard, was done in the studio. The orchard was such a low set that it was very, very hard not to show the banks of lights. I had to hang shreds of imitation sky over it, blending one with another to hide all that equipment. Menzies created the whole look of the film; I simply followed his orders. Sam Wood just directed the actors; he knew nothing about visuals.

Objective Burma! was also shot entirely in the studio; we just stuck tropical plants in the foreground of each shot. Nobody knew what radar looked like in those days so we got an old bedspring and fixed it up, and that was supposed to be radar! Two pictures of that time I didn't enjoy working on were *The Hard Way* and *Confidential Agent*; they were both directed by tiros, new men, and I wasn't happy with people who in my opinion didn't know the business.

Generally speaking, I found working at Warners during the forties hard work, with four pictures a year, and often uncongenial work as well. Jack Warner had hired me because he liked the way I photographed Hedy Lamarr in *Algiers*. He wanted me to shoot low key because he was concentrating on that as the studio look; I was put under a seven-year contract.

I had a very big problem with *The Time of Your Life*, from the Saroyan play about a bar. The whole thing took place in the bar and there was a mirror all around it on all sides, so it was very hard to hide the lights and the camera. I devised hanging lights finally, but it was terribly hard.

One of the very best pictures I have done was *He Ran All The Way*, directed by John Berry, who was blacklisted, with John Garfield and Shelley Winters. It was the story of a criminal who holds up a family in New York. It was very, very realistic; for an indoor swimming-pool scene we actually got right into the pool with swimming-trunks and used hand-held shots through splashing water. I used only what daylight came through and a very few natural lights in the foreground to fill in the shadows. We got enough reflection from the water to give their faces texture; if I had put too much light in it would have washed out the faces. That's the danger in many films of overlighting, over-correcting. Of course, some stars wanted the light very bright, to wash out their lines!

We had a tiny apartment in *He Ran All The Way*, exactly copied from a real one; we put the camera in a wheelchair and pushed the cameraman around. On *Body and Soul* I myself got on roller-skates to shoot the boxing scenes and they pushed *me* around. I wanted an effect where the boxer is knocked out and he looks up into a dazzle of lights; with a heavy, fixed camera, you'd never get that.

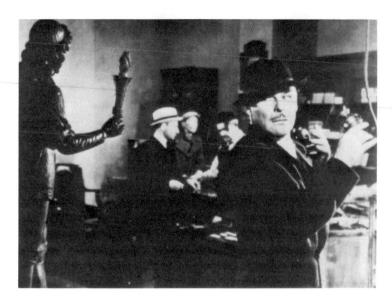

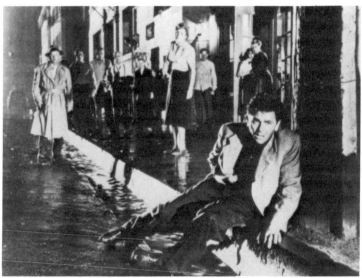

(*above*) Brian Donlevy in *Hangmen Also Die*; (*below*) Wallace Ford, Shelley Winters, John Garfield in *He Ran All the Way*

Floyd Crosby started work on *The Brave Bulls*, showing the early training of the bulls; he had done the same for Norman Foster and Orson Welles on *My Friend Bonito*. Crosby and Robert Rossen didn't get along, so I took the picture over. I built a harness and had it mounted on one of the real bullfighters; it was sixteen millimetre, quite small, with a good wide-angle lens. You could see his cape moving in front of the camera and the bull charging him. The camera moved with his movements; the bull horns almost brushed the lens. Then I took a bull's head and mounted it on the handlebar of a bicycle. We took the bicycle and charged Mel Ferrer, who couldn't fight bulls. The camera was mounted on the seat of the bicycle; it shot through the horns. You felt you were the bull now. I cut to and fro: matador's point of view, bull's point of view. You swore it was all real.

We dug a pit and fixed a trapdoor on it near the bullring. When the bulls ran out we'd lift the door and shoot through the hooves. It was hot, stifling down there. And we never knew exactly when the bulls would come. So I had a telephone installed in the pit and we would get the cue. Every now and again we'd come up for air when they'd give us the all clear. It was hell, but fun! I loved the Mexican light, with its brilliant contrasts, its dense, black shadows. It gave the picture a very strong look.

The best scene in *Picnic* was the one of the picnic itself and the dance between Bill Holden and Kim Novak. I found some Japanese lanterns and I put a little spotlight above each one with different coloured gellos in front, and I had the dancers moving in and out of the colours. It was all shot near Hutchinson, Kansas.

I was supposed to photograph *La Duchesse de Langeais*, with Greta Garbo, which Max Ophuls would have directed and James Mason was to co-star in. Walter Wanger called me up and asked me to do the tests of Garbo at the Chaplin Studios. I expected her to come with a large entourage, but she just strolled in and asked where the dressing-room was. Rollie Totheroh, whom Chaplin had left in charge, said that it wasn't too clean, and asked her with an air of surprise where her make-up man and hairdresser were. She said she'd do it all herself.

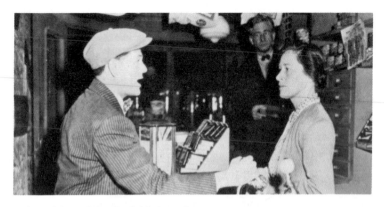

Body and Soul: John Garfield, Anne Revere

She came out all done up by herself in a big floppy hat, slacks, and a white blouse. I had never photographed her; I was frightened. This great lady! She asked me what I wanted her to do. I arranged a table and I put a column up. I said, 'Well, maybe you can lean against the column.' She said, 'If I lean against it, can I smoke a cigarette?' I said, 'Sure.' She leaned against it, and started smoking, and when the camera started to turn – it was a silent test, so you could hear the camera noise – she listened to the grinding sound and her face changed, her expression, her whole emotional mood came to life and transformed her completely. It was incredible, wonderful. I had started out with just general lighting, but she inspired me, and suddenly I found myself changing lights, changing everything so as to make that 2,000 feet of film really memorable. She was like a horse on a track: nothing, and then the bell goes, and something happens. When the shot was over, she said simply, 'Have you got enough?' And I said 'Yes,' and very matter-of-factly she remarked, 'OK, I go home.' She did. And she was nothing again.

I directed a couple of pictures around that time: *Go, Man, Go,* and a picture about Dong Kingman, the Chinese painter. *Go, Man, Go* was about the life of Abe Saperstein, and how he found and

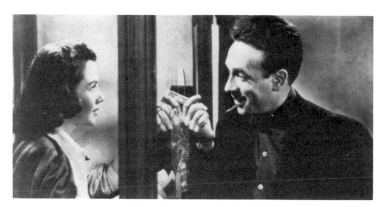

Go, Man, Go: Pat Breslin, Dane Clark

developed the Harlem Globetrotters. I went to New York and made the picture on a twenty-day shooting schedule; it was quite good. We had a problem with the scenes when they travel around by car; we couldn't afford process shots. We took the wheels off the touring car and set the car on a trailer chassis, so there was room to put the camera on as well, then we drove around. But we had a problem because the trailer's diesel made a shattering sound and drowned out the dialogue. So we'd go to the top of hills, and let the trailer chassis go without the engine, and off the whole thing would go to the foot of the hills. So the Globetrotters were always going downhill in the picture! That is what's so good about low-budget pictures; you have to use your ingenuity, your imagination. The whole thing cost 130,000 dollars. It cost that much to put in power-lines and telephones for *The Molly Maguires*.

Sweet Smell of Success was exciting; it was a pleasure to work with Sandy Mackendrick. I used varnish to give the look of the film a glitter, in the bars, many of them real in New York. I used very small bulbs; photoflood effects worked well because we had so much polish on the walls it made everything shine. The whole film shimmered; few films have that look. I used the same effect in two or three places in *The Heart Is a Lonely Hunter*.

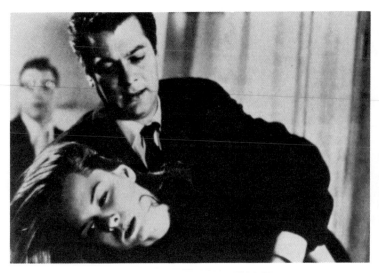

The Sweet Smell of Success: Susan Harrison, Tony Curtis

In the sixties, the films I have most enjoyed doing have been with Marty Ritt. I suppose *Hud* was the best of them. All the exteriors and all the interiors except for the ranch-house were shot in Texas. When Mr Ritt called me on the film he told me I wouldn't be happy with the background stuff they had already done; it was very flat, nothing but blank skies, no trees, and he asked me if I could double print clouds to fill in the blankness. But when I got down there, and saw those harsh skies, that flat glare, I thought, it has a certain beauty; I told him that just what he didn't want was picturesque cloud after cloud. So when I saw a cloud I put a filter in to take it out, instead of the other way round; the sky came out very light, and washed the clouds away.

There was one shot I liked particularly, in which Paul Newman and his young brother were standing in the backyard and the light was coming from the porch. They were drunk and they were near a water-trough. I used incandescent lights; I took condensers out

Hud: Patricia Neal, Paul Newman

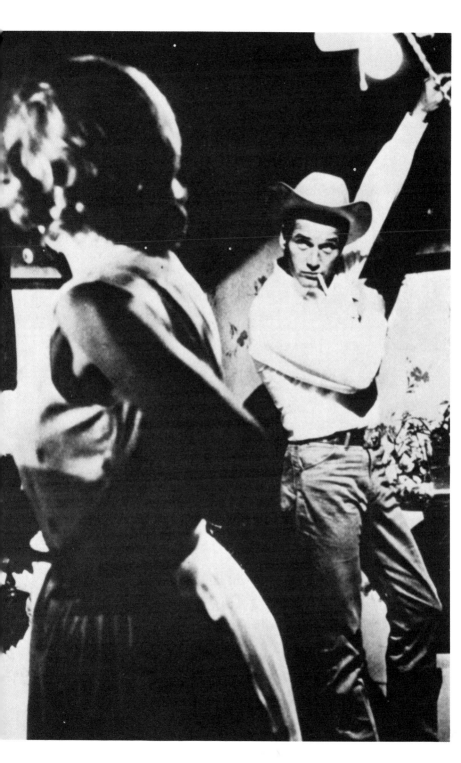

for the interior arcs to flood them out more and get sharper shadows. I was very, very happy with that picture.

I didn't like *Hombre* as much. *The Outrage*, a remake of *Rashomon*, was slightly better; but the opening scene on the railroad station should have been on location. The studio had a backing done that was very artificial, very bad. I did a bad job too; I'm ashamed of it, but I just couldn't figure out what to do with that badly painted backing. The moment I put the light on it you could see what it was. Rain is the hardest thing in the world to light. It doesn't show up unless you backlight it. The camera moved 360 degrees at one stage; and that made it very hard to backlight. Sometimes I could only light half the rain, and it would blur away at the bottom of the frame. It was very uneven visually. And the results were no good. We should have used a dust-storm and done it on location.

I'm proud of *The Molly Maguires*, very proud. We shot it over five months in the coal-mines of Pennsylvania, and we rented a number of houses occupied by retired miners. We had to 'date' the story, so we covered the nearby highway with dirt, coal-dust and so on, and repainted the houses, and put power-cables in for telegraph-poles. Television antennae were all removed. We re-created a whole landscape; Tambi Larsen, who did *Hud*, was the art director, and he is very good. Unfortunately, the front office wouldn't let Marty Ritt shoot it in black and white.

I went down into the mine about 1,200 feet; we couldn't work down there, because it was dangerous, and very cramped. Larsen took impressions of the walls and re-created them in the studio, with the aid of 200 tons of coal. When you walked in it was exactly like it was. It was a difficult lighting problem because the people's faces were black with coal-dust and they had a tendency to blend in with the coal. Just luckily, there was enough reflection from the coal to give some relief. I had to crosslight a little, but that was hard because the only source of light in the mine was from little oil-lamps, worn by the miners on the front of their caps, or set in little niches in the walls. We had to have just enough light to see the faces, see the expressions, without cheating. For the exteriors,

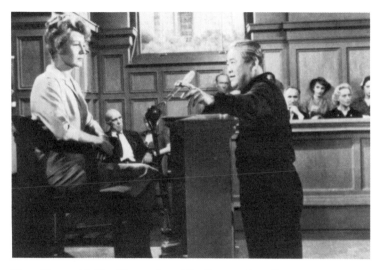

Wong Howe with Rita Hayworth on *The Story on Page One*

I had a man spray the greens with black, so that you had a black landscape, and men picked the buds off the trees.

I didn't use a single arc in the whole picture. I used quartz lights, which are just coming in; they are very small units, which was lucky for me because I could get them out of camera range in the mine. There are a couple of shots lit with just one tiny quartz globe and nothing else. It's about the size of a peanut. It was a great challenge, and I loved it. Of course, the new fast Eastman film was a godsend in getting an exposure. We nursed the film and nursed it, because it was just out and there wasn't much available. There wasn't enough to go around, and we couldn't waste a foot; we shot to cut – about 400,000 feet. We made the film deliberately roughly; it's not polished at all. If a light got kicked we just left it that way out of place; it gave odd yet interesting results.

And, like Stanley Cortez, I enjoy odd results. Off-beat things, unpredictable things. I believe they increase realism. And realism comes first with me, always.

5: Stanley Cortez

I've always maintained that colour photography – and we in Hollywood can only talk in terms of colour, now that black and white is dead – should not be naturalistic, that one should always feel free to make mistakes. We have so often had to follow the studios' specific styles. I remember that M–G–M and 20th used to fight; Louis B. Mayer saw one of Zanuck's pictures in the early days, and Mayer decided to change all his pictures from soft to hard colour as a result, and told Karl Freund and his other cameramen what to do. The other studios followed suit. So as a result we got 'Christmas package' colours in Hollywood films of the forties and after – a distorted sense of colour values in which everyone wanted to put more and more colour in.

Nowadays, we are getting the opposite problem: purism, a classical approach to colour. In those days the colour was too bright, now it's too dark, but in neither case have most cameramen here been bold, gone out to try new things. Even though a thing might be technically wrong, to me that wrong thing can be *dramatically* right. To hell with all this caution! To hell with this 'academic' approach! You must *distort* colour, play around with it, make it work for *you*, intentionally throw it off balance. You can mirror emotions in colour. There are times when nature is dull: change it.

Sometimes people here try to experiment, but when the top brass see the first day's work, they criticize it. They say: 'What the hell happened here?' In one picture I made recently, *Blue*, I had a sky—a strange, purplish, blackish thing. The remark was, 'Gee whiz, this looks like something for a typical musical comedy.' Then I thought, 'Maybe I was wrong?' And four nights ago I looked up at the sky in Los Angeles and it was exactly the way I had it on my filter. Mine was a *dramatic* concept, not a realistic one. I have always insisted on this over my producers, my directors. Of course very few of them have the faintest idea of the miracles that go on all the time in the field of optics.

In *The Bridge at Remagen* I changed nature by making everything fresh and bright look instead almost monochromatic: bleak greys and browns and umbers. It was a war picture, and the greens of summer were fresh. I dulled them to keep the mood grim, warlike. I seldom have a fully preconceived idea about how I am going to light a film. I simply experiment all the time.

And anyway, who knows what's involved in a picture until they try something out? For instance, to get a so-called 'low-key' effect you have to use an enormous amount of light. I remember doing a picture called *Eagle Squadron*. We shot it with Plus-X film, and where normally our exposure would be 3/5, I exposed at f/16. It was a time when Leon Shamroy, Arthur Miller, Gregg Toland and myself were the four cameramen in Hollywood going for depth of field. Gregg used special Waterhouse stops: pieces of metal with small holes inserted in the lens, and I did, too. So *Eagle Squadron* was an experiment in Tolandesque techniques, and very interesting. And as so often, in that picture I put the key light on the floor, or any strange place, rather than in a fixed spot, which they so often do in Hollywood.

Every day I consider something new about light, that incredible thing that can't be described. Of the directors I've worked with, only two have understood it: Orson Welles and Charles Laughton. Most directors don't even know what the end photographic result will be in terms of light, because what appears to the eye does not necessarily appear on a photograph. What the eye responds to, the film does not. There are limitations in film, unfortunately.

I was born in New York City, and I'm as enthusiastic about

living as the day I was born. My people are Middle European, my mother was born in Hungary and my father was born in Austria. My father was a designer of men's clothes, and, oddly enough, my childhood ambition was to become a conductor. Life wasn't too easy; we weren't people of tremendous means, and you can imagine New York before World War I! I think my photographic eye was formed very early, when I was a small child, and became aware of what was going on around me in my little street. I used to look at the stars for hours, at the rain in the gutter, and dream about things. Everything mystified me and attracted me. I was curious when other kids were not. I saw things they didn't. I wouldn't play games as much as the others. I would often be by myself, and just watch and listen to the sounds and the sights of a thousand things.

Indirectly, I think I was preparing myself from the very beginning for what I am today. I always had a strong visual sense. I started out in New York as a designer of studio settings for photographs, then as an assistant to great photographers who specialized in photographing men in elegant clothes. I worked with children's photographers and portraitists. I got ten dollars a week and learned all the time.

One day I was taking a walk on Fifth Avenue and I saw there was a parade going on. I was in front of the Public Library when I saw a man cranking a camera. Everyone else was watching the parade, but I was watching *him*. He was evidently trying to puzzle out why I should do so. His name, I found out when I spoke to him, was Van Der Beer. He worked for Pathé News. He learned of my interest and got me a job on a Pathé serial in New York. That gave me a break. From there I went to Paramount as a novice, working for Bert Edlington, head of the Camera Department (he was later at R–K–O).

Out here in Hollywood I worked with Alvin Wyckoff, who was De Mille's cameraman, and my first job was on a picture starring Thomas Meighan. At night, I would come into the studio and quietly work on the movie camera – my job was strictly fiddling with lights. I wasn't supposed to touch the camera. But in those spare hours I'd crank it, see what made it tick. It fascinated me. I was so young! I gave myself five years to be an assistant, five years to be a camera operator, and five years to establish myself as a first cameraman. And it all came true.

When I finally started shooting I was the youngest first cameraman in the world. I was twenty-six years old. The picture was *Four Days' Wonder*, and I have forgotten it. But I do recall making a kind of two-reel thing as a director, called *Scherzo*. It was 'way out', with trick lenses and false perspective; I was involved on it with Slavko Vorkapich, who influenced it deeply. You could call the film cubistic. Rather like *Ballet Mécanique* in style. The subject-matter was, simply, water. Water and again water. We showed the birth of water, the fragmentary beauties of water in raindrops, streams, puddles. It cost me just 500 dollars to make. I shot it here, down the coast of Mexico, Miami Beach, at Santa Monica, all over.

Unfortunately, there was a fire and the negative was destroyed. There may be one or two prints in Europe somewhere, but I don't know where. What a sad thing . . . it was a symphony of light: I had all kinds of reflections in glass and so on, refractions and deflections, and a man called Rosenfeld did the music. I never did that kind of thing again.

I was assistant to many great men: Karl Struss, George Barnes, Charles Rosher, Charles Schoenbaum, all at Paramount. And to Hal Mohr, as well. Joe August, Arthur Miller . . . I did films that were shot in twelve days, quickies, at Paramount; we had fun, we never worked by the clock at all. I remember Alan Ladd was doing bit parts in those days. I did things for Albert Rogell and Otis P. Garrett. I started to acquire the beginnings of a style.

I used to love working in the thirties with Busby Berkeley. I was his camera operator on that scene with the hundred girls and the hundred pianos. He used to sit around for days at a time, and we'd play cards just because at the moment he wasn't quite ready to unleash some new imaginative idea. We had all the time in the world then. And the studio had complete faith in this man. Finally, he would decide on the formations he wanted with me

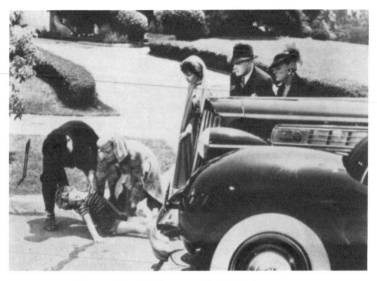

The Forgotten Woman: Donnie Dunagan, Sigrid Gurie

and with George Barnes, my mentor – who also taught Toland, by the way. I met Bus originally on pictures made for Sam Goldwyn: *Roman Scandals, Palmy Days,* musicals with Eddie Cantor in the lead.

I went to Universal in the thirties, where they let me handle all the off-beat subjects. In one picture I did there, the story dealt with a subway train which existed in a New York station long since closed down and forgotten. The tunnel had been filled in, and the carriages became the lair for all kinds of strange subterranean people. A very strange, fascinating film with which I could do quite a lot of off-beat things photographically. It was based on a true story.

I was always chosen to shoot weird things like this. I remember *Forgotten Woman,* with Sigrid Gurie. She was a nurse, looking after crippled children. I used a photographic technique there in which I tried to penetrate the thoughts of the nurse, by showing them

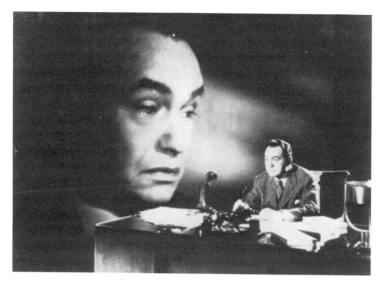

Flesh and Fantasy: Edward G. Robinson

inside her head. It was quite new. I made one of her eyes completely fill the screen – that was entirely new then – and in the eye I showed the reflection of all kinds of thoughts, so that you were looking through the eye as through a telescope into the recesses of the brain. I used coloured lights for this black and white film so as to achieve striking contrasts within the iris, the white of the eye. And sometimes I'd show an ear or a nose or a mouth, just to isolate a feeling she was having, in which one organ became particularly paramount. I used sometimes beads of water that would have the same look as eyes . . . I went on and on. It was wonderfully rewarding, to be able to experiment like this. Of course, people said I was much too arty!

On *Badlands of Dakota*, I used infra-red film to create an effect in black and white, for a rather strange sequence in a graveyard. It took place in the early morning, and we wanted a rather sinister and off-beat feeling. *Eagle Squadron* certainly had a lot of interesting things photographically; it was directed by Arthur Lubin, and Diana Barrymore was in the cast. I shot night for night, which was very, very unusual then; and I had some very, very close shots. I remember I said to Diana Barrymore, who was reading a book – the close-up of her was one of the biggest ever – I said to her as she reached page 34, 'Miss Barrymore, you are merely *an inch* from the lens. Would you kindly stand back?' We laughed and laughed! We also had a remarkable scene visually in London, when she meets her lover on a bridge. We had lions and shimmering lights and just enough fog so you could still see the outlines of the surroundings. I did something similar in the *Lord Arthur Savile's Crime* episode from *Flesh and Fantasy* later on. Another remarkable feature of *Eagle Squadron* was that some of the aerial stuff was actually shot in England, very rare in Hollywood war pictures. Then it was matched in with an extraordinarily complex series of trick shots, miniature shots, process shots, and so on. The film as a result wrote history in realism; it was remarkable. It came, of course, after *Ambersons*, and developed many ideas from that.

Needless to say, the whole business of *Ambersons* is fascinating to think about today. I was at Universal when I met a man called Ray Clune, who was production manager for Selznick. He gave me a chance to make some tests for Selznick; David saw them, and engaged me to work for him; I did tests of Alan Marshal, Gregory Peck, Joan Tetzel, and others who became part of his stable. While I was working at R–K–O, Welles was preparing *Ambersons*, rehearsing it; I had access to the stages, a privilege at that time. Welles was on Stage Three, and he had eight sets upstairs and downstairs, and Orson was rehearsing on all these actual sets. And I said to myself, 'I'm sorry for the guy who has to photograph this damned thing.'

There was a man who was very close to Orson called Jack Moss. He was a great magician, and helped Welles learn magic. Jack mentioned to me that Welles was going to use an R–K–O camera staff. I said, 'That's fine, they're all good.' But meanwhile Orson had seen some of the stuff I did at Universal: *Danger On The Air*,

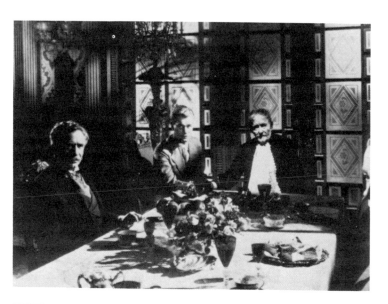

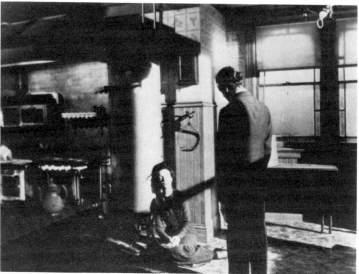

The Magnificent Ambersons: (*above*) Ray Collins, Joseph Cotten, Richard Bennett, Tim Holt; (*below*) Agnes Moorehead, Tim Holt

The Black Cat, and so on. And the tests I made for David Selznick. After talking to Jack I went to New York for David to make some tests for George Cukor. While I was there, Jack called me and asked me what I was doing in New York. I said, 'What do you think I'm doing?' He said, 'Orson wants you to do his picture for him.'

I didn't know Orson Welles from Annie Oakley. This was on a Friday night. Of course, I was anxious to do it, even though I didn't like the idea of working on those enormously difficult sets. I had to find David in New York. How? It was Friday night, he could be anywhere. Finally I located him at the home of Henry Luce. I told David about the Welles call. David said, 'Are you satisfied with what you've done for me so far?' And I said, 'Yes.' He asked me if the man who was working with me could follow along the lines of the same style. I said, yes, and we called Los Angeles from Luce's. Over the phone we agreed on a contract – Selznick, Welles and myself. I left New York Sunday, arriving in Hollywood Monday at noon. I met Orson Welles for the first time in my life on the Monday night on the set, and we started shooting Tuesday morning. I had no chance to make a test of anybody.

You remember the opening scene I shot? It came well into the picture, and it showed the family at dinner. Joe Cotten made a speech about automobiles. I shot the scene, feeling tired after the all-night flight, and I saw the thing through the lab that night. I was pleased with the negative results, and Mark-Lee Kirk's superb art direction showed up well. But the positive is something else again, and when we all assembled to see the first day's work we were all so on edge; me especially . . . to fly from New York and start straight away, my God! Then we saw it and Orson was delighted. He put his arms around me and he told me I was 'in'. Immediately, there was a *rapport*. From then on to work with Orson was a fantastic experience.

He gave me complete freedom, but every one of his suggestions was of enormous importance. We did the sleigh scene in an ice plant, downtown in Los Angeles on Sixth and San Pedro Streets,

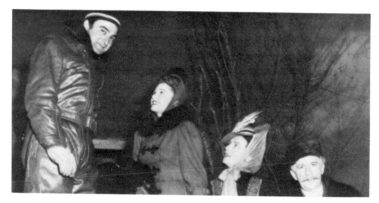

The Magnificent Ambersons: Cortez with Anne Baxter, Agnes Moorehead and Ray Collins 'in the ice plant'

where they used to keep meat and other perishable goods. We built the set inside the ice plant, and I tried to get the feeling of Currier and Ives prints. We used the ice plant chiefly so that we could show the breath of the people on the air. We were there for ten days, as I recall. We had to wear long, fur-lined, leather-covered suits, and swig brandy, to keep the cold out. It was a most difficult thing, because the lights would break . . . we used 5,000 watt, 10,000 watt, and they shattered in the cold. I used a lot of arc light on the snow, throwing it in at an angle to suggest sunbeam glare. There's a certain purity in the light that I wanted.

For one sequence, when the camera explored the Amberson mansion after everyone has left it, I took the shoes off my operator and with a heavy Mitchell camera he walked up the stairs with it and through the rooms. We used a periscopic finder, and a thirty-one-inch lens. He had to move, we had to 'choreograph' him like a ballet dancer as he walked so the weight was not unbearably heavy.

In another shot we went through six or seven rooms. When this was being discussed during rehearsal, before I had been hired, I said to the cutter, Bob Wise, 'Wouldn't it be wonderful if that could be done in one shot?' Orson must have overheard me because when we came to do the scene, he said, 'Can we do this whole scene in one?' I said, 'Orson, we can, if you're ready to gamble with me.' We did it; every time the camera went through a room, we saw four walls and a ceiling! Walls moved on cue, and in went a light on a predetermined line, all while the camera is moving. It was a symphony of movement, noise notwithstanding!

It gave the actors a little bit of a problem because they were trying to do their acting in the midst of all this going on. I remember that to add to my problems, some rooms even had mirrors. They had to be turned around on cue and turned back on a second cue, on hinges. Each room needed a different kind of light and had a different kind of décor.

Harry Wild and Russ Metty did some scenes, I remember. Russ photographed the ending in the hospital corridor under the direction of Robert Wise. Harry Wild photographed the scene in the railroad station, done in a kind of forced perspective.

Orson had a radio show to do. He couldn't always find the time to direct certain scenes personally, so he would pre-record his direction on records, and leave me with the camera crew to direct some scenes, or leave them to me and Bobby Wise. The sequence for instance in which Dolores Costello is reading the letter; the curtain is blowing; there are some interesting shadows. I had some unusual lighting effects to point up her eyes, and her tears, as she was walking. Bobby directed the scene to Orson's recorded directions, as it were.

Charles Koerner, who came to the studio after George Schaefer, the studio boss who hired Orson, resigned, was a distribution boss originally at the New York end of R–K–O, and he was obsessed with the idea of the double feature. He came out with the arbitrary edict that no film left the studio longer than 7,500 feet, no matter what the picture was. He put *Ambersons* into that category, which was so wrong. Of course, as a result, an hour of my best work went, magnificent things, shots involving new small arcs I used for the first time.

Aggie Moorehead was so wonderful in that picture. Every time

I see her in the street I creep up behind her and whisper harshly, 'George!' just the way she did in the picture!

Aggie was also in *Since You Went Away*, which I did for Selznick: a very interesting picture about the women, the families at home in the war. George Barnes was supposed to do it, and I was due to go into the armed services. I got a call from Ray Clune to say I was to take over from George. I didn't want to do that; I used to work for George, as his operator. So I called George and asked him what the problem was. There *was* one: I can't go into the story, because I worshipped him and do still, although he's dead, God rest his soul. I redid most of the scenes he did, I'm afraid.

It was a very important and costly film. We built a whole house, front, back, everything, fully furnished, to house the family around which the story was told. It was a masterpiece of set design, without question. I was fascinated with the whole lighting problem in the film, and went on and on shooting, so long in fact that I had to go into the army as a buck private, I missed my chance for a commission! Finally I *had* to go into the army and Lee Garmes finished the picture. We got co-credit; actually, I did most of it, as Lee will confirm. The opening scene, showing the interior of the house, the bulldog, the rain, the fold-out portrait of the husband, was shot by George Barnes, superbly. I did the big hangar dance scene. The great shot of the whole hangar framed in the wings of the American eagle was a split-screen shot. We used the same railroad station they used in *Gone With The Wind*, by the way.

Smash-Up was an interesting experiment: a film about a drunk, with Susan Hayward. We had a scene in which the heroine is lying in bed and mumbling; she's having a nightmare, and I went to my doctor to ask him what happens in a person's mind when he is drunk. He told me about the flashing of lights across the brain, and I had lights actually *inside* the lens; and I conducted a kind of symphony of light over her. As she reached a pitch of distress I raised the lights to the highest pitch possible. Susan Hayward helped by actually getting drunk to play the part! I didn't

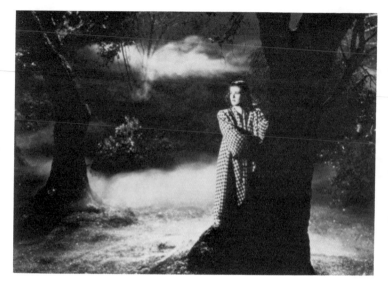

Secret Beyond the Door: Joan Bennett

want to do the cliché thing and show her distorted impressions, but rather convey her thoughts with abstract play of lights alone. It was fantastic.

I also did one or two things in Fritz Lang's *Secret Beyond The Door*. I used an elaborate interplay of light. But even more weird was *The Man On The Eiffel Tower*, directed by Burgess Meredith, who took over from Irving Allen. We climbed the Eiffel Tower girder by girder, and at one stage Franchot Tone actually risked his life. To get out of the lens for one particular shot he had to walk behind a railing on to a tiny narrow ledge with a drop of about 100 feet below him. He had to hang at one stage by his fingers so that he wouldn't be in a particular shot. He was very brave. The film was released on Ansco Reversal film, and it looked odd. It went through nine emulsions, and I was none too pleased.

Apart from *Ambersons*, the most exciting experience I have had in the cinema was with Charlie Laughton on *Night Of The Hunter*. I had photographed a film with him – *Abbott and Costello Meet Captain Kidd* – and we became close friends. Charles and the producer Paul Gregory came out to the set of my picture *Black Tuesday* and Charles told me about *Hunter*, and asked me if I'd like to do it. Of course, I was delighted.

Every day the marvellous team that made that picture would meet and discuss the next day's work. It was designed from day to day in fullest detail, so that the details seemed fresh, fresher than if we had done the whole thing in advance. I used to go to Charles's house every Sunday for six weeks before we started and explain my camera equipment to him piece by piece. I wanted to show him through the camera what these lenses would and would not do. But soon the instructor became the student. Not in terms of knowing about the camera but in terms of what he had to say, his ideas for camera. He was very much influenced by Griffith; we ran all the films Griffith made.

We had a scene with a little boy in bed. We showed shadows on the wall. Charles wanted to dolly in on the child, to discover him. I suggested we start with a close-up of the child and then pull back to show the mysterious quality of the room gradually. He agreed at once.

Perhaps the most extraordinary thing we did was the shot of a drowned girl in a car under water, her hair streaming. We used a wax dummy for Shelley Winters. I tested the tank at the Fox Studio, but it just wouldn't do, because the paint kept coming off the sides. Finally we used the tank at Republic. I hauled in a huge crane from which I suspended a platform, and powerful arcs that would penetrate the water to create that ethereal death-like something you had in the water. We used two cameras, one actually in the water, the other shooting through glass. We engaged Maurice Siederman, who did *Kane* and *Ambersons*, to do the hair and make-up on the Winters dummy. We had to create a current in the water to make the hair stream out, without your seeing the current at all. We used wind machines. The underwater cameraman was dressed in a scuba diving outfit, and we had an effect in which the camera

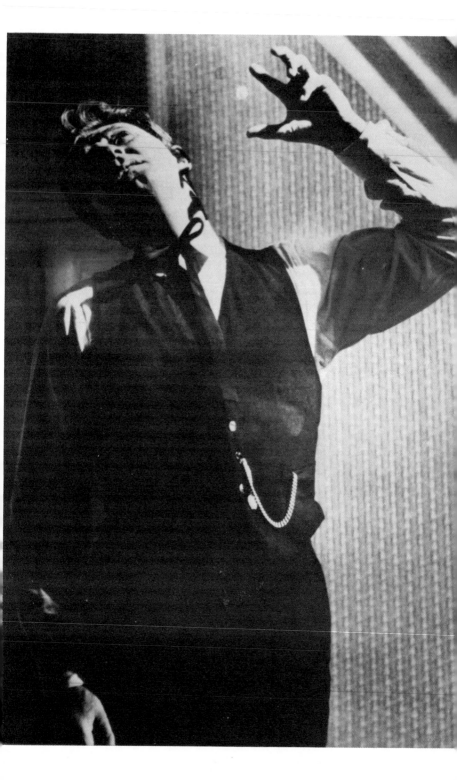

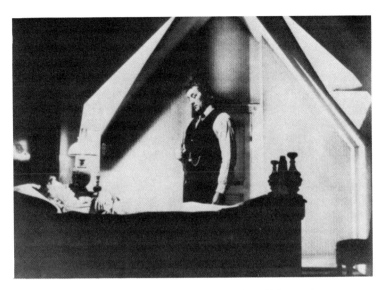

(Above and opposite) *The Night of the Hunter:* 'Valse Triste . . .'

is on a hook under water and it tips up and follows a thread, up to the boat. Do you know what it means to do a shot like that? We had another cameraman under water with the first man and he kicked him in the fanny and up he went along the line to the bottom of the boat! I painted the thread white so it would pick up the contrast.

The death scene with Bob Mitchum and Shelley Winters was something I was very proud of. Shelley Winters is lying in the foreground and Bob Mitchum is in the background, and without a sound he goes through a series of strange positions in relation to her before killing her. We had an A-shaped composition formed by roof-beams, and I lit the whole thing with just five lights. Charles must have seen something on my face, something strange, because he looked at me very hard and said, 'What in hell are you thinking of right now?' I said 'None of your God-damned business,' in the nicest way. But he insisted. And I told him – music is

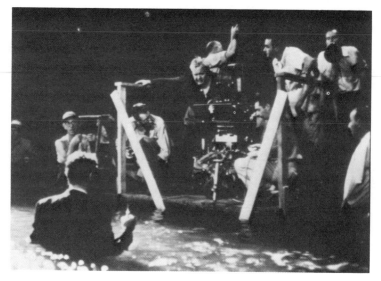

The Night of the Hunter: shooting the prelude to the river sequence, with Mitchum in tank, Laughton centre, Cortez to right of Laughton

my hobby – I was thinking about a certain piece of music. He said, in his own typical way, 'Pray may I ask what was that music?' I told him it was Sibelius's 'Valse Triste'. He turned white. 'My God,' he said, 'how right you are. This whole sequence needs a waltz tempo.'

He sent for the composer, the late Walter Schumann, and I told the composer what I was doing visually so that he could interpret it musically. I often will revert to music as a key for a photographic effect.

People to this day ask me where we did the scene of the chase along the river. We used a tank on Stage Fifteen – and when I tell them that, their faces turn white; because it looked like a real river. In the scene when the two children are on top of the hay-stack and in the distance you see the mother by the light of the moon, we used some very elaborate tricks. But better still was the scene of the child in the loft, looking down and seeing the preacher in the distance; we built the whole set in perspective, between the hayloft and the fence, which was about 500 feet away. The figure moving against the horizon wasn't Mitchum at all. It was a midget on a little pony. The lighting gave the illusion I needed; the feeling of mystery, of strange shadows. And I even used an iris: on the boy at the window. Charles wanted to crane in on him, but I used the iris instead.

Charles and I worked together for eight months on a projected version of *The Naked and The Dead*. An exhibitor from Philadelphia named Goldman was to have financed it. Spencer Tracy, Montgomery Clift and Burt Lancaster were planned for it; I spent weeks and weeks in the Hawaiian Islands location hunting; Terry (who had directed two scenes of *Night of the Hunter* in Ohio) and Denis Sanders were brought in to condense the film and bring down the budget in pre-production. I was associate producer.

On *Black Tuesday* I used for the first time in the history of the screen Tri-X film, as an experiment to give a harsh, grainy look. In one shot in that I had every light turned out on the set and lit the whole thing with a single candle! It was the only source of light, and the candle cast a beautiful light on the face of the star, Jean Parker. It has never been done before or since, to my knowledge. They sent the film specially to Rochester so that the Eastman people could look at it. Of course, I always turn the 'stage lights' off on a sound stage so that I can see everything with my eyes alone. We shot four or five sequences in a meat-packing plant. It stank, it was horrible. The producer, Goldstein, came down with some people to show off, and when he got there the stench stopped the show!

Samuel Fuller is someone I have worked with often in recent years. He used to carry a pistol around and fire it. He has quietened down now, I'm glad to say. He's a very sensitive man.

We shot *Shock Corridor* in sixteen days. It was a brutal picture, and I tried to give it a brutal look. *The Naked Kiss* is about a sex pervert, a harrowing thing for which Sam Fuller used his own home as a set. We had some good things there: I remember a

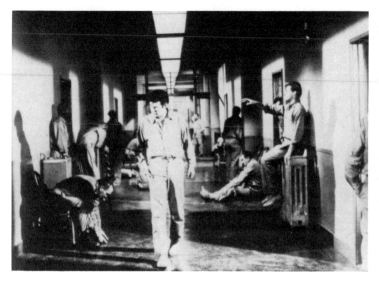

Shock Corridor

scene in which Constance Towers is coming down a line of beds, and we used some unusual effects of light and shadow; even though I say it myself, it was a magnificent sequence.

Again in *Three Faces of Eve*, as in so many of my films, I was given an off-beat subject, a psychological subject. It was about a girl with three personalities; I read the script thoroughly, and oddly enough I backed out of treating each episode with a different photographic technique. I told Nunnally Johnson, who wrote and directed it, that Joanne Woodward must *play* the whole thing, that everything depended on her, that we couldn't help her with lighting.

Finally, Nunnally came up with the idea of her putting her hand in front of her face at the end of each scene to indicate the change of characters, and of the three acts. She looked up, and she was different. All I gave her was a very subtle change of light as she went from one person to another. I saw the film that two

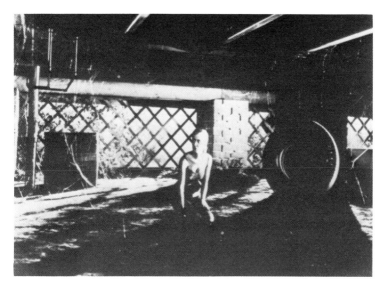

Three Faces of Eve: Joanne Woodward

doctors – this was a true story – had made of the actual patient concerned, and with the assistant director, when Nunnally Johnson was ill, I actually directed a couple of scenes, based on that medical film. Joanne and I looked at it often, and I will say that Joanne's performance was far superior to the actual patient 'playing' for real! I toasted her at the end of the shooting party in champagne and told her she would win the Oscar. She said I was insane. She won it.

Of recent films I have done, I'm particularly proud of *Blue*. Judd Bernard approached me to do the picture for Silvio Narizzano when, at a cocktail party, Curtis Harrington recommended me to him – so I became involved through a martini! The part of Blue, the half-Mexican, was to have been played by Robert Redford, but he bowed out. We ran into trouble with Terry Stamp's accent, which damaged the picture; they brought him back for redubbing after the previews, they went to England, and did more; and they still didn't get it right. And all he spoke was 200 lines of dialogue in the whole picture.

I wanted the most fantastic cloudscapes anyone had ever seen, and I think I got them. We were lucky. The picture was shot at Moab, Utah. We selected the locations by helicopter, and they were marvellous; the whole of the opening scene, when a number of riders gallop through a township, was shot by helicopter. Then the camera becomes a rider and rushes across a valley, through clouds of dust. It was quite a problem keeping the riders together. The two side horses were ridden by assistants in Western gear with walkie-talkies who communicated with the others and kept them in the frame.

In another scene the camera hurtles through tall grain; I was proud of that. We wove through it without cutting much of a swathe; we wanted to ride through it with the camera, as though the audience were riding. So many good things were in that picture, but so much went for nothing; I don't know why. The picture cost between four and five million, largely because we were on location for eight weeks. It flopped.

Following *Blue*, I made *The Bridge at Remagen* for John Guillermin. Whereas *Blue* was a poetic, rich work, the more recent film is a semi-documentary example of realism. There is an overall deliberate drabness in this film, a look of grim war, with primary colours forced out. When the men are on their way to the bridge to blow it up, which is their mission, they learn that they haven't just got to blow it up, they have to take it by force. This meant sacrificing leave for four days.

From that moment on, I decided to change the whole photographic concept, to parallel the change that had overtaken them. I spoke to John, and he agreed that once these men realized their changed mission, we should switch from fixed to hand-held cameras. The jerky hand-holds would convey their nervousness, to involve the audience in their uneasiness. John went for the idea, luckily.

We blasted away a whole mountain, we built a huge church on top of a mountain, and we did a fantastic amount of work in

Czechoslovakia, until the Russians came in, and suddenly we had a real war on top of the one we were faking. We had to get out in a terrible hurry; I'll never forget the strain. We went to Vienna, and then to Germany; we had to reconstruct the whole thing, and leave some of our best interior shots behind. In Hamburg we rebuilt the whole interior of the tunnel we had originally built in the Prague studios, and spent seven weeks reshooting. We had to rebuild two-thirds of the bridge we'd built in Czechoslovakia in Rome and everything had to match. We even had to match shots to those we had done in Czechoslovakia of a reconstructed German town. We shot night for night, and I was wounded in the hand and the foot in the tank scenes.

I shot in every kind of light, every kind of weather. We had many, many cameras, and nine Czech cameramen whom I had to address through an interpreter. As I sit here and think of it, I wonder how I met the challenge. But challenges I love. Now I'm looking for the next one. Have another Scotch?

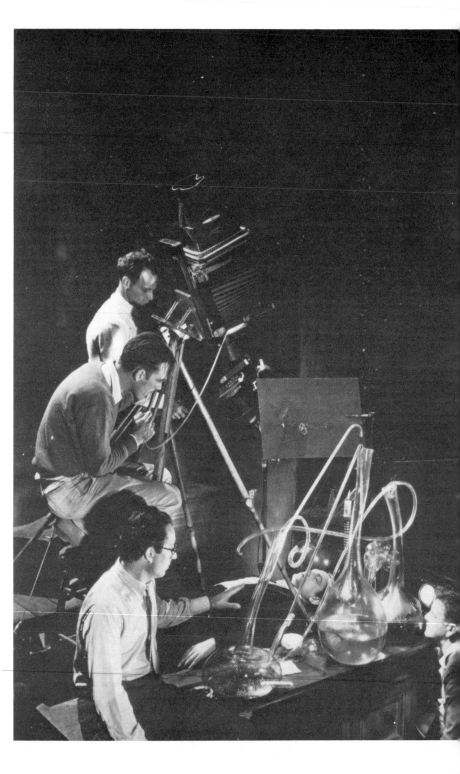

6: Karl Struss

I was born in New York City on West Seventy-third Street, and I was the youngest of six children. There were three sisters and two brothers, and then of course a father and mother! I went to public school and high school, and in my last year at high I had pneumonia so bad I couldn't take the exams. My father told me to get to work. I was in his factory ten years, and I hated it. So I took up photography in self-defence. My father was originally the owner of a silk-mill. The panic of 1892 put him out of business and he went into manufacturing bonnet wires, wires covered in cotton and spun silk. I had to run those awful bonnet-wire machines. I was on my feet ten hours a day, from sixteen to twenty-six years of age.

I went to Columbia University night classes after work. I travelled to Europe on vacation at the age of seventeen and by that time I had two cameras with me. I had already experimented with a soft-focus lens with a camera on a tripod. I also used a small portable camera. Then I began building low-price soft-focus cameras; a firm which made submarine periscopes did my aluminium mounts. I advertised in a magazine that began publishing my photographs, and I sold my models, which were more practical than most. I somehow scraped together the money to get the best engravers and printers in New York, and eventually I opened a little studio on Thirty-first Street where I did portraiture, magazine and advertising illustration.

Dr Jekyll and Mr Hyde: Mamoulian (*left*) and Struss (*right*) in foreground

At night after all those hours standing I'd work till all hours developing once I had left college. Every one of the films had to be swabbed with absorbent cotton to make it right. It was exhausting.

After World War I, I came out here to California. I went around the different studios, to Famous Players-Lasky where Mr De Mille was, and a young guy there called Horwitz showed an interest in my work. He knew De Mille wanted to do still studies of the stars, but not with the director of photography, who up to that time had always done everything. So here was my chance.

I got a contract for three years with Mr De Mille. When he went to Europe on an assignment the contract wasn't renewed for some reason, and I went into the independent field. Mr De Mille would always say, if he didn't like my work, it was 'Death Valley for you and no water', but he did have respect for me. Like all the other directors, he knew little or nothing about lighting, and left the lighting to me; his main concern was getting performances out of the actors.

In those days we were using orthochromatic film, and blue eyes came out as 'fish eyes', and yellows were black. I started using panchromatic film when nobody was using it; I experimented, and I was able by using the panchromatic and filters to change the look of, say, Gloria Swanson's dresses from one shade to another in black and white, which avoided actual costume changes. I took the whole thing to the head of the Camera Department at Paramount Studios, and they were very impressed. Later I used colour filters in black and white to show the healing of the lepers in *Ben Hur*, and the changing of Dr Jekyll into Mr Hyde and back again in Mamoulian's picture. The most fantastic thing I ever did was in a picture at 20th with Margaret Livingston, *Hell's 400*, in which there was a scene involving the Seven Deadly Sins.

I had the Sins dance around her in colour, with her face painted grey and her clothes grey and everything grey. Of course the whole sequence was done in colour, but we *painted* everything else to make it look as though it was in black and white. You could do things like that, then; you *could* be a painter.

When you photograph someone and change them into some-

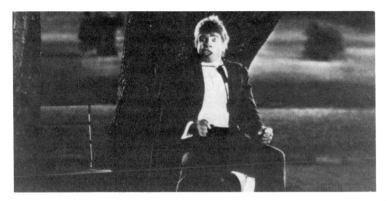

Dr Jekyll and Mr Hyde: 'They made him look like a monkey . . .'

thing else without cuts or dissolves (as with March from Jekyll to Hyde), you have to put red make-up on the actor's face. Then, when you put a red filter on the camera, it doesn't show the red make-up at all. The lips of course remain the same, so they are painted a neutral grey. You move the filter up or down very slowly, and as it moves, you see the make-up emerge. I worked it out for Mamoulian. I thought they made a very bad mistake; the change from Jekyll should have been largely a psychological one, with subtle changes only in the make-up. But they foolishly changed the hair and put false teeth in, and made him look like a monkey. That was terrible. Jekyll's shouldn't be a physical change, after all, it should be a mental one. The worst scene of all showed him watching a couple of midinettes dancing in a cabaret and he was scratching himself like a gorilla. Just awful.

I was with Paramount for eighteen years. I worked with Louis Gasnier – he had a fine photographic sense, very fine – and Thomas Ince. I think *Ben Hur* was the first picture I could do a lot with. I worked on the picture for three months in Rome; entirely with Christy Cabanne, a top director then, and a graduate of Annapolis Naval Academy. We started to prepare the chariot-race when the ground was frozen in the cold days of March, and in the grandstands

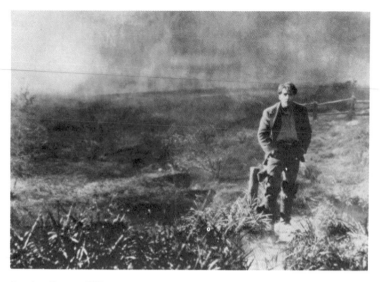

Sunrise: George O'Brien

they had puppets, a quarter of a mile away; 7,500 of them, working on strings! We never actually shot it, though, in that way. Then the company ran into some trouble with the Italian Government, and had to hurry to get our negative out as fast as possible. Later, in Hollywood, I photographed the scene of the lepers, and the scenes in the streets of Jerusalem. When the lepers were healed we showed a glow of light on Christ's hand and we used a green filter which showed the leprosy make-up, which was painted red. Then we changed over to a red filter and the red make-up did not show, so they looked healed. Of course, there were several other cameramen on the picture, including Clyde de Vinna.

I rather liked *Sparrows*, with Mary Pickford. Miss Pickford had lots of children and there was a swamp and lots of alligators and a farm. I remember we had to shoot directly over the alligators, and it was very dangerous. We put enormous gauzes in the trees, thirty by sixty feet; and we had three in a line. They all had to be backlit,

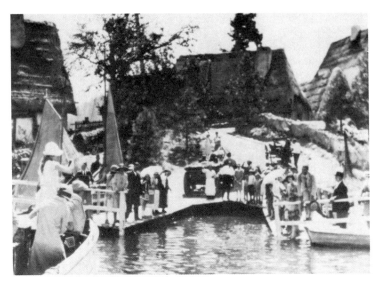

Sunrise: ' . . . as we dropped down, a group of people arrived by boat'

and we used special reflectors. Miss Pickford was always shot through gauzes, but this was something else again!

Sunrise reunited me with Charlie Rosher, who did *Sparrows* with me. Most of the time we worked together on *Sunrise*, but there were several occasions when I did the shots solo. The toughest one of all that I did on my own was the one where George O'Brien is lit by the full moon, shining through the fog; my camera was a Bell and Howell and Charlie's was a Mitchell, and he couldn't shoot the scene with his Mitchell. I could do it with mine: the dolly was suspended from the studio ceiling, and it was on a curved track, and it had to come down and take in the boy and trees and water, all on the stage. We had to swing over to the right and show him walking towards the camera. We followed him on through the trees.

We had this mass of trees in front of us and the camera had to 'punch' through the trees. When we got through them the girl was waiting for the boy and powdering her nose. In those days the film would only run up to 200 feet and had to be cut to be developed then. This scene ran about three minutes and we were turning the camera at sixteen frames a second. I had to change film practically in the middle of a shot while at the same time seeing the image upside-down in the finder and reversed and not losing the visual thread!

We often shot towards the sun to create a shimmering effect. We did many of the lake scenes up on the northern shore of Arrowhead. I did one week's shooting there when Charlie was sick; I did one very complicated shot in which I had the camera on an elevator and started high, and as we dropped down a group of people arrived by boat.

All the sets were built in perspective. I remember when I first came on the set I walked across to where the girl was standing in a doorway; she was small, and the top only just came over her head. And across the hallway behind her was a door only three feet high! The art director, Rochus Gliese, did a superb job. He was a real Prussian, he clicked his heels. The dance floor I remember was on a slope, again in perspective.

We had an extraordinary thing there. The boy is standing thinking, and the girl's on the bed, and slowly on the wall beside the bed you see there is a little movement. The movement gradually gets brighter and brighter and goes up higher, until he is eliminated and we are out in full sunshine. That took about a minute. Mr Murnau wanted a lap dissolve, but I thought of something else. I made a graduated gauze filter which started with one thickness and then two and three and four and five and six thicknesses until it was blacked out. I started with it blacked out and all you saw was darkness, and then I lightened the filter; of course all you were seeing really was sunshine all the time, from the start of the shot, but it was only revealed gradually, and looking into the darkness you *thought* you were looking into the wall, naturally. That was all my idea, my shot, not Rosher's. Murnau left the whole visual side of the picture to us; he concentrated entirely on the actors. Of course, he'd see what size the image was, and he was interested in the permanently moving camera; he had a certain feeling.

One of the opening shots was in a village at sundown. We showed lights coming out of doorways; to achieve the effect of interior light coming out and the twilight, the soft light around it, we had to work without exposure meters; there weren't any then! Today it's all mechanized; then we were artists.

Oddly enough, a friend of mine was with Murnau and his chauffeur when they drove to Santa Barbara; they were going at ninety miles an hour, and this friend of mine had had enough; he got out. And then just after that Murnau was killed in that terrible smash.

After that I started work with D. W. Griffith. He was receptive, a good man, though he was then past his peak. *Drums of Love* was set in a South American country, with an imaginary royalty, and it was about a woman who married an old hunchback, played by Lionel Barrymore. She fell in love with his younger brother, and he discovered them. William Cameron Menzies designed superb sets. I also did an experimental short with him based on the '1812 Overture'. We showed Napoleon on a horse, and with an arc of unusual power projected his silhouette on to an enormous screen, and the soldiers marched by with this figure towering over them.

Battle of the Sexes I saw again very recently; it was dated so bad! *Abraham Lincoln* had Walter Huston; he got better as the picture went on, I thought. It was straightforwardly shot. It was an episodic affair, by its nature. There wasn't much you could do with it.

On *Night Watch*, which I did for Alexander Korda, we shot an awful lot of it in a tiny eight by ten cabin on a battleship, with a full ceiling and pipes in perspective. It was one of the first times full ceilings were used. *Kiki* was one of the first films of Betty Grable, who doubled for Mary Pickford in long shot in the dance scenes.

I was assigned to Mamoulian for *Dr Jekyll and Mr Hyde*. To suggest the hallucinations of the man as he changed, we had the assistant on top of the camera whirling around, and changing the focus. I suggested the handling of this. In the opening scene, we

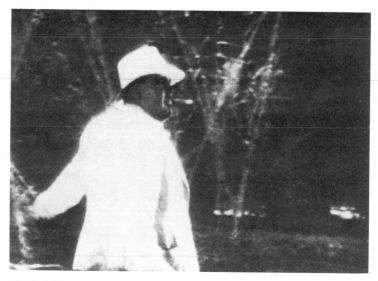

Island of Lost Souls: 'Laughton was superb as Dr Moreau'

had a fantastic thing: the camera begins by showing March playing the organ, we had a briar pipe coming out of the camera, and smoke going up, the camera started on the organ tubes and went up and then down to the hand that was playing, and then it swung around and took in the valet and went into the carriage, via a hallway and then into a lecture hall. I used an oval gauze with soft edges, and when he went into the hall I tried to make every shot of every student look like a portrait.

The Sign of the Cross was, of course, a great challenge. I used gauze throughout, to give a feeling of a world remembered; it wasn't much used then, as it had been in the silent period. I shot the whole black and white picture through bright red gauze. That goat's-milk bath scene was horrible to shoot. It got so sour after we had been shooting it for a while, oh boy, it smelled to heaven! It was there for a week. Claudette was really nude, so she couldn't get out too often. She suffered!

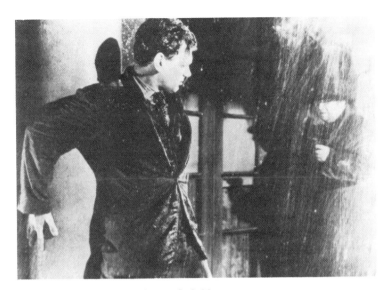

Journey Into Fear: Joseph Cotten, Jack Moss

Island of Lost Souls was an interesting thing. Erle C. Kenton who directed that had been a pictorial photographer, and I had met him when I was exhibiting stills in the early twenties. We actually went on a steamer to Catalina and shot the picture on it, with the half-human animals whimpering on board before you get to the island where Charlie Laughton was the mad scientist. The cages were out on deck. Luckily, we had a real fog, which was called for by the script. I had a subjective camera shot there again, as in *Dr Jekyll and Mr Hyde*, when the evil doctor is murdered by the creatures on the island, and he looks up and sees the vivi-sectional instruments over him in a kind of forest of steel. I admired Kenton; he had a greater command of the English language than anyone I ever worked with. He played every scene through for the actors, even for Laughton, who was superb as Dr Moreau.

I very much liked working with Mae West. She was charming.

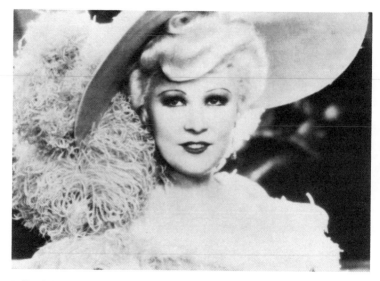

Belle of the Nineties: Mae West

In *Belle of the Nineties* she wore magnificent period gowns, and I did a series of portrait studies of her in it, based on my work at the beginning of the century. They won't let you do that today; the people have to move, the camera has to move, always, and the directors try to do the job themselves. I also did *Go West, Young Man* and *Goin' To Town* with her; in *Go West, Young Man*, I had a shot that went right through the audience and up into the stage where Mae West is appearing in a theatre, and then she takes over the action. As in *Jekyll and Hyde*, it was all in a single take.

In the late thirties, Charlie Chaplin's brother, Sydney, called me. His usual cameraman, Rollie Totheroh, couldn't handle *The Great Dictator*, which Charlie was about to make, and so Sydney asked me to do it. Later, on *Limelight*, they did start out with Rollie Totheroh and a top crew, but Rollie still didn't know how to light. So they called me in on that one, too.

Limelight was slightly the more interesting of the two films photographically. I wanted to use two cameras for every shot, which we had done on *Dictator*, but he wouldn't let me do that the second time. I thought I'd help him, give him something to cut, because he had no knowledge of camera direction, his films were completely 'theatre'. It was very routine work with him; you'd just set up the camera and let it go and he and the other actors would play in front of it. He never even tried for cinematic effects. Once or twice I'd tell him I was going to do my best to make a move, so I'd have a slide up to a window and the camera move into a room. It takes time to set those things up, but he would come in at ten – he always started work at ten – and say that we were being much too slow. Well, for Gosh sakes!

Journey Into Fear, which I did for Orson Welles, was a very different experience. Welles and Foster, Norman Foster, who directed it, worked together for several weeks before Welles went to Brazil to make a documentary. We did one scene that took forty-nine takes, after midnight, just a tiny shot of Welles and his shadow at the bottom of a gangplank, then he climbs it and goes on to the ship. No one could really say whether Take Forty-nine was any better than Take One. It was all so extravagant and crazy!

A lot of the picture was set at night. And much of it was on a ship in the blackout; if you shot too low you'd see there was no ocean there and if you shot too high, you'd see over the top of the set. It was very difficult; we had long travelling shots that never seemed to end; and you had to do them in near darkness, moving cables all the time. Once they wanted me to have a cabin with no lights at all. Mad! How could you develop it?

The Macomber Affair, from Hemingway's story, was a lot easier. We re-created Africa in Mexico. Every day we drove to the location in taxicabs sixty miles over terrible dirt roads. Tyres kept blowing up. We somehow managed to sneak the camera into a jeep to shoot from inside it. I don't know how we hid the lights. Zoltan Korda wasn't at all like his brother; he was rather phoney. I remember we were looking for a location where the lion was to attack Robert Preston, who played a cowardly hunter. I wanted to

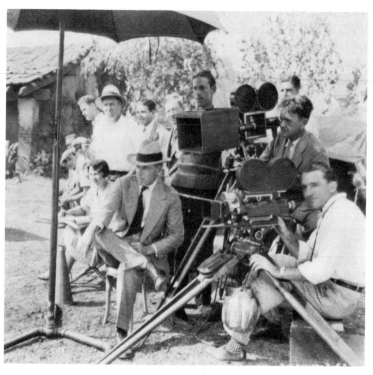

November 1927: D. W. Griffith seated, Struss at camera, on *Drums of Love*

get a steady build-up of shots leading up to the scene and I carefully selected the angle where the sun would fall. I remember he made me change everything, and then we wound up with almost the identical effect anyway. I don't think he knew what he was doing. Another time we shot all day in one place and suddenly that night Korda almost casually announced to Peck and the others that he would do the whole thing all over again the next day. It was completely pointless, and the second day's shooting was exactly the same as the first except for some tiny gesture of Greg's!

I made the first 3-D picture, in Italy, with Toto. It preceded *Bwana Devil*. We had two huge Mitchell cameras, and they were quite a problem. Also in Europe, I did *Attila the Hun*, which had so many directors and so many cameramen, there seemed no end of them.

The Fly, which I did back in Hollywood, was just plain ridiculous. There was one scene there which I told the director, Kurt Neumann, was crazy. They had the figure of a man reduced to the size of a fly, and the fly talked. And they made the man say, 'Help me, help me!' in a tiny voice. Oh, gee! It was as bad as the monkey Hyde. I did a lot of science fiction at the time; *Rocketship XM* was especially good. I used special lenses to create a distorted feeling in the space ship, and I had some wonderful planetscapes in outer space, with fantastic cloudscapes; I went hogwild with filters.

Lately, I've been doing commercials. It keeps me busy. Of course, a lot of the directors don't know what they're doing. But you could say that of some feature directors as well!

7: Arthur Miller

I always gave a director my best even if he was a truck-driver. The basic principle I have had in making pictures was to make them look like real life, and then *emphasize the visuals slightly*. If we had a Childs Restaurant with white tiles in a scene I'd show it even more white and shining on the screen. I'd make everything as sharp and clear as possible. Of course, an audience's eyes can't adjust from dark scenes to bright ones immediately, so in order to consider the pupil of the eye I would always work a gradual change of light when you came into the restaurant. From daylight to a brilliant interior with soft shades of grey in between.

When I did *How Green Was My Valley* with my favourite director, John Ford, we had a scene in which the audience is taken from bright sunshine into the black hole of a mine. In order to show the change gradually, I talked Jack into shooting the scene so that we would stop at the pay office, where there was just a little more shade, and lead the audience slowly into the darkness. After some argument Ford saw my point, and later he pulled a switch on me; when a man comes out of the mine later in the picture, he made me show him suddenly blinded by the intensity of the light. Of course, that was completely right dramatically.

I was never a soft-focus man. I like the focus very hard. I liked crisp, sharp, solid images. As deep as I could carry the focus, I'd carry it, well before *Kane*. There were no secrets in our crew, at 20th, in the good days. When we used an effect everyone knew

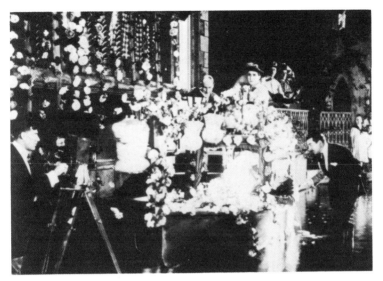

Arthur Miller left, behind camera, George Fitzmaurice right, filming *Bella Donna*

exactly what the diffusion was, the intensity of each arc. And we'd work right in with the electricians . . . I had the same gaffer for eighteen years and in the end we'd just have to look at each other and we knew what we were going to do. There was no need for words; we were like a lot of dummies all through shooting.

I tried my damnedest to get light to come from natural sources; sunlight through blinds the way it is in Eastern places for instance: you recall *The Rains Came* and *Anna and the King of Siam*. Of course you need grading as well as realism: for instance, *The Lion in Winter*, which I saw recently, is one of the most beautiful pictures I ever saw, but it has a fault, it's *too* beautiful. It's like walking through the Louvre and at first you see a Picasso and you want to study every brushstroke, but after an hour and the fifteenth picture you might as well be looking at the *Saturday Evening Post's* cover. Douglas Slocombe's every scene in the film deserved an Academy Award, but the overall effect is so beautiful it's boring. It wears out the eye. It cancels itself out.

I always tried to avoid a monotonous succession of beautiful shots. I'd have a drab one in between. And I always liked simple effects. For instance, in *The Birth of a Nation* Billy Bitzer had no proper lights at one stage, so for a street scene he just used one lousy sun arc right up at the back of the set, plumb in the middle, and it made a beautiful pattern. That's the way to do it: improvise, invent.

I was born in a place called Roslyn, Long Island, which was a very small rural town about fifteen miles out of New York, across the East River and out of Queens. I lived there till I was about five, I guess; my father was an engineer and he put down what they called macadamized roads, before asphalt and all that kind of thing. I guess it was just crushed rock and it was on rollers, and he'd lay out the route and so forth.

He moved to Boundbrook, New Jersey, and built a stone-crushing plant for the road company. From there he went to work for the Otis Elevator Company up in Hartford, Connecticut, and for some reason he opened the door on the ninth or tenth floor of a building when he was fixing an elevator, stepped in, there was no elevator there, and he went down the shaft, and that was the end of my dad.

I have a brother who was with a Wall Street broker. I had some trouble at home and left home and went to work on the race-track. In 1905 I had a severe accident that knocked me out of the business. I was in hospital for four months and when I got out racing was over in New York. I met a guy who ran a horseshoeing plant and sold hay, grain and seed, and traded in horses. I worked for him, putting the tag on a horse's rump when it was sold and delivering them, riding bareback and leading another. I knew a bookmaker named Adam Kessel, and one day I was talking to him outside a beer-garden when I saw some people who looked like they were making moving pictures. I made little Brownie No. 1 pictures myself and had a dark-room on the race-track and made pictures of the horses, so I was interested in what they were doing.

A fellow came over to me as I sat bareback on a horse and asked me if I wanted to work in moving pictures. I asked him, 'Doing what?' He said, 'You can ride a horse bareback can't you?' I said, 'Yes.' And he told me, 'Well, we have about a week's work.' I went back to the fellow I was working for and took a vacation, and I went to the studio, on Fourth Avenue and Third Street, in Brooklyn. It was in a German beer-garden – not much of a studio, just a platform really with cantered sets, and in the beer-garden there was a stage where they ran movies and showed cheap vaudeville plays. Under the stage, you could just about stand upright, and we would develop our prints under there at night. I met a guy called Fred Balshofer, in 1908, and I was curious as to how they developed the long Brownie film with six or seven exposures. Balshofer seemed to know and he took me in the studio laboratory and showed me. (In the meantime, I'd ridden horses in cowboy pictures – that was all they made then – including one called *Young Hero of the West*.) Balshofer showed me about developing, but he was suspicious of me: he thought I was some kind of weisenheimer trying to find out too much at a time when Edison and the ruthless patents companies were fighting a battle for camera rights.

We started to make pictures under the brand of New York Motion Picture Live Pictures. We were afraid to make pictures in Fort Lee, the then heart of the motion picture business, because of the detectives over there from the Patents Company. So we went down to a place called Jamaica in New York State. We were on the waterfront there making a picture about a fisherman's daughter and two others when – I forget at what moment exactly – a fellow told us we could have a scenario for nothing if he could play the leading part. I thought he was terrible: it was called *A Son's Loyalty*.

Something odd happened to me during these pictures: I had always been a little runt and suddenly I grew a whole foot. Whether it was the change in my material circumstances I don't know! (On the race-track I lived on peanut butter, crackers and tea!) I worked on a picture called *Davy Crockett*, as an assistant cameraman to the 'conductor', which directors were called then.

In 1918 I made my first trip to California and we rented space out at the Universal Studios. I began photographing films with full credit: things with Fanny Ward and Lewis Stone. I began to like the sunshine and decided to stay. In those days this was a gorgeous place: no smog, orange and lemon groves: paradise. You never had such a thing as a 'weather permitting' call; you could call 3,000 people for June 21 on a location up here at, say, Harrison's Ranch, and the sun would be up there, fully guaranteed, at six o'clock that morning. It always rained from January through March, then it quit and never came back until the next January. Just glorious sunshine day after day after day.

The studios were lovely places with trees and fresh grass. Pepper and orange and eucalyptus trees grew around them . . . today they hate grass and trees. They've gotten so they hate anything beautiful: those goddamned places are nothing but concrete and lousy old buildings. I had to go back in 1919 to New York, because George Fitzmaurice, the director, wanted me; we were on the payroll of Famous Players-Lasky. I stayed with him right through until 1925. He was a talented man until talkies; he was only a man of the silents. He couldn't cope with the change. He was a real artistic person. He had all the patience in the world when he tried for something real or something on the art side. In those days all the art directors came up from the carpenters' shops: art to them was a hammer and a nail. Art directors as such came in somewhere around 1915, but they had no background, so the director had to create a picture with the cameraman.

Fitzmaurice's speciality was in designing a film beautifully, and in handling women stars with great flair. He could do a beautiful love-story very well. He had the ability to get the best out of women, to get along with them.

I think *Peter Ibbetson*, which I did with him, was wonderful, the best picture Elsie Ferguson ever made. It is lost forever, they can't find a print of it. The title they gave it was – inappropriately – *Forever*! It was my first big chance: the story of a woman who

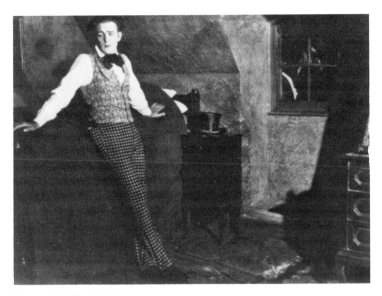

Forever: Wallace Reid

comes back as a spirit. This fellow practically sleeps with this spirit. We didn't use the usual double exposures with a transparent person running around. We brought them in and let them go with a wisp of smoke only, and the lighting did the rest, to make the figures look less than solid. A Hearst black and white artist worked alongside me and gave me a lot of advice; he taught me the whys and wherefores of portrait photography and composition. We broke completely new ground with this: up to then ghosts had looked so darned corny.

Then I made *Bella Donna*, the story of a poisoner in Egypt, from the novel by Robert Hichens. This very building we are sitting in belonged to the leading man, Conway Tearle. The studio we made it in was down here on Vine Street. We had a boat on the 'Nile' with Pola Negri and Tearle. We were short of palm trees for the tank so Tearle said to me, 'Go up to my house and ask the gardener to take all the potted palms in the garden, they're set around a

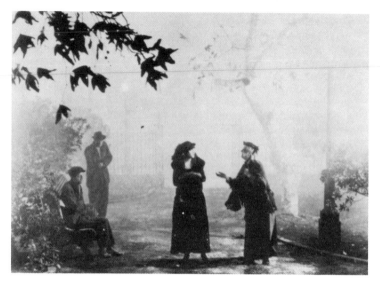

Bella Donna: Pola Negri

pond.' So we loaded the palms on to a truck and took them down and we put some of them on the boat itself. . . .

It was Pola Negri's first picture in America and I was worried. In asking me to handle her visually, the director wasn't any more specific than if he'd been a music-teacher asking for a 'pear-shaped tone'. But I was used to this. A director like that was all right; others would try to tell you exactly how to handle a scene. To get along with them you'd have to hear them out completely, of course, but all the time they were telling you something they thought would work you were formulating something that *really* would work. I made Pola Negri look all right, I guess.

After working with Fitzmaurice, working with De Mille was uncomfortable: on *The Volga Boatman.* It's terrible to talk about a dead man this way, but I never met such an egotist in my life. Even when he was wrong and knew it, if he said it it had to be. Panchromatic was first coming in then, and for night shots you had to use red filters, but the trouble was it made the faces come out white. So I developed some make-up. And with panchromatic you had the advantage that you could make blue skies look dark. I told De Mille we could get some tremendous effects, so he told me to make some tests, and I did: of an old boy escaping with a haywagon. It was wonderful stuff: you'd see the wagon silhouetted against a hill and yet the sky was black, so you'd get the authentic feeling of moonlight. I even made oil-derricks look like palm trees! I was wildly enthusiastic, and I told De Mille how we could get wonderful shots of the actors' faces against poplar trees swaying in the wind. And we'd do the close-ups in orthochromatic where necessary. He agreed, and when we started to shoot I was all ready to switch the films around in the camera.

Suddenly De Mille blew up and said he didn't understand me, first I wanted ortho, then panchro, what the hell did I want? After Fitzmaurice this was impossible. I said to him, 'All I want, just this minute, is to be let alone for Christ's sake so I can get this shot of the boat being pulled up and I can then turn the camera round, put on some orthochromatic film and shoot down on the water and get the streak of the light on the water.' After that nothing I did was right. The rushes came in and were shown in a little theatre up the Sacramento River valley. There was nothing stronger than a candle behind the projector and when I saw *The Merry Widow* there you saw nothing on the screen at all! So for the rushes I rigged up a device to give more light. But De Mille still insisted on dragging us all out of bed at three a.m., forcing us to drive a hundred miles to a bigger theatre to have a look at the film. Right then I lost my respect for this man forever.

Around that time I did a picture with Spencer Tracy. The director was a stunt-man and half-loaded. He wanted to do a duck-shooting scene at daybreak, four o'clock in the morning, and I recalled that I had done a similar thing back in Inglewood, New Jersey. I dug it up and found an old notebook which told me what stock I used. Spencer Tracy said to me, 'We're shooting those sequences in midday sunshine. How the hell can we make it look like four a.m.?' And I said, 'It'll be all right, Spencer, I'll do it.'

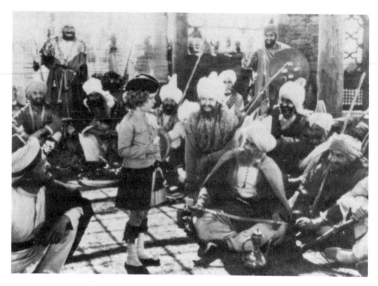

Shirley Temple in *Wee Willie Winkie:* 'I used a lamp on Shirley that made her whole damn image world famous'

And I took the light test illustrations I had made all those years before and blew them up and used them again, matching them in with the new stuff.

Came the sound period, and I guess I became best known at first in connection with the Shirley Temple pictures. She was a most delightful child, who spent her childhood with grown-ups – my crew at 20th. We were a family together for years, and we played games with her: we were a kind of police force and I was the captain. We wore caps and badges. She loved it, and we became kids again. She not only knew her own dialogue – her mother coached her – but she knew everyone else's in the cast as well, and when her adult co-star blew a line, she'd know what he'd missed and she'd say, 'You were supposed to say so and so.' It drove her mother crazy and as for the actor . . . oh, my God!

I always lit her so she had an aureole of golden hair. I used a lamp on Shirley that made her whole damn image world famous.

It was a lamp that everyone uses now in television. The light doesn't hit you direct. It had a 250-watt bulb in it with a special piece of metal on the front of it, so all you got on her was reflected light. I had a little rheostat and I'd play a little game with her as I'd turn the light up and down. I always kept the key light up, well over her eyeline, two feet up, and I'd always surround the camera itself with black velvet, and she'd look right into the black velvet, even on exteriors. And I'd light the actor she was talking to under normal, so she was in high key and he was in very low key; this gave her the star build-up, you see.

I used the same technique later in *The Song of Bernadette*. I'd have the actors look down a little in that one, too, while Jennifer would look up. You often cheat that way.

In *The Rains Came* I had to handle Myrna Loy. Now there was a problem on that picture: Clarence Brown was from Metro on loan to Fox and he didn't want the cameraman they had given him. He wasn't 'brilliant' enough. Bert Glennon was his name. Zanuck said to me, 'Tomorrow at noon, walk in to the set with your own gaffer, your own regular crew.' They had been shooting the great scene of the Maharani's dinner-party; Brown, who had been an engineer and was a smart cookie, a smart director, wanted the whole thing to shine. And Glennon had made it shadowy and soft. So I walked in at noon, and Brown said to me, 'The trouble is we aren't getting enough light, enough brilliant sharpness, and I hope you and I can get along.' And we did, and Glennon walked off.

So I said, 'O.K.' And he asked me if I wanted to do my own tests of Miss Loy. And I said, 'I've already photographed Miss Loy.' He said, 'You have?' He was surprised; and she had forgotten: it was when she played a vamp in a Loretta Young picture. She asked me before we did the test to have a matchbox light with a red gelatin on it shine in her eyes with fifteen candle power. I thought, 'What the hell was the use of that when I already had hundreds of watts shining on her anyway?' And I asked her what she wanted it for. And she said, 'It makes my eyes dark.' Crazy, of course, but I jiggled it around for her and whether she had the light and the gelatin on it or not didn't make any difference! It

143

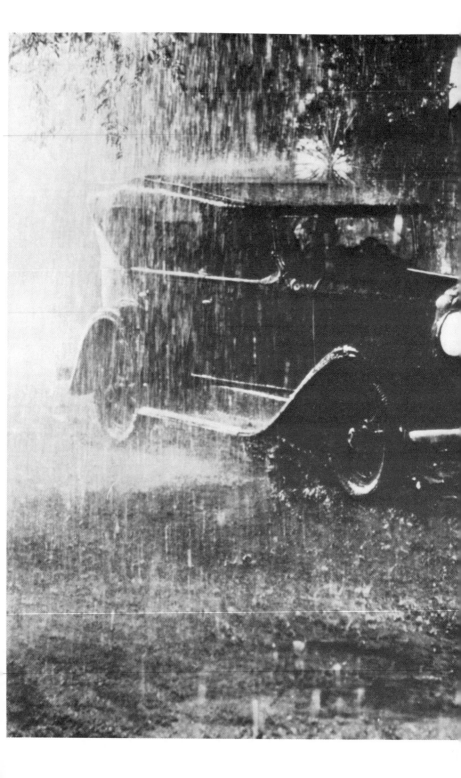

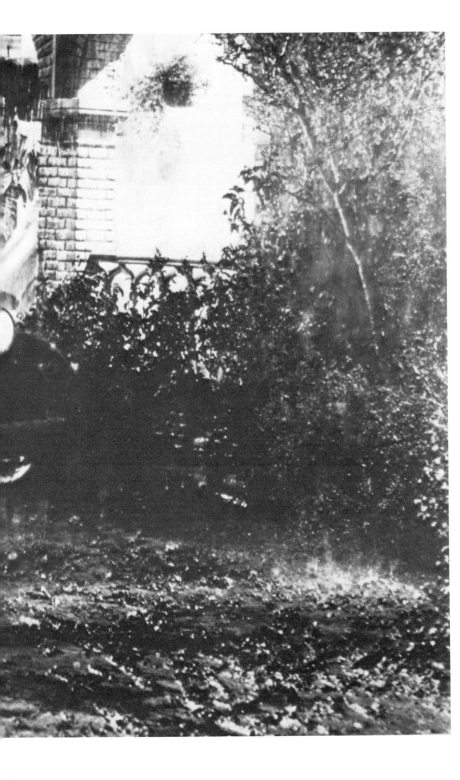

was all hokum; stars get that way. Luckily, she accepted my point that the light she wanted had no sense, and from then on we got along O.K.

But oddly enough, I did use the red gelatin once. It's when she takes a drink in the hospital and you know she's become infected with a disease and her face fills with shadows. I just wanted a special kind of look in her face, as though death is coming over her and she doesn't know it. And the gelatin was wonderful for that.

I got the 'brilliant' look that Brown was after, and it was the sort of thing I was getting known for, which is why he hired me, I guess. I sprayed all the tables with oil, and the silverware was polished and repolished. When the old Maharajah died and the veil over the bed blew a little in the wind, I made the whole scene glow as vividly as possible, to suggest a spiritual, transcendent quality.

I became obsessed with rain on that picture; I was always amazed when I left the studio that it wasn't raining. I hate movie rain that falls straight down, and I know that rain never does; it always falls at an angle. I made the prop department adjust the spouts accordingly. I even shot the raindrops so they seemed much larger. Oh my God, you never saw such water in your life! Brent and the others took a hell of a beating on the picture. There was one scene when Nigel Bruce and his manservant were on the landing of their house and the water rushed in and 'drowned' them in one shot, without a cut. And in fact the actors actually took the full force of that, and even had bits of the set flying on to them! They risked their lives, even though the material was balsawood; if it had hit them the wrong way it would have killed them instantly. . . . When the storm breaks for the first time a curtain billows out and you see the hard shadow of a lattice-work printed on it. I got the effect with a hot sun arc busting through a lattice-work.

One trouble with the way they handle rain today, in television for instance, is that they don't backlight it. You have to backlight rain or you don't see it; it's just a blur. And all the way in my picture the rain shines; it was the theme of the film.

I guess in that picture I really 'got' my style of having shadows hard and very bright highlights indeed, with the furniture heavily oiled. Of course, Gregg Toland used heavy contrast in *Citizen Kane*, but I never liked his style in that (people think he invented 'Waterhouse stops', where you narrow down the focus without the automatic iris, which we had before he and I were first working). He only succeeded in distorting the faces, and I don't think you should distort them. You don't see people that way, and I like a degree of realism, at least. He was after realism, but he didn't achieve it.

After *The Rains Came* I went on to *The Mark of Zorro*, with Mamoulian. I liked him, he let me alone and didn't bother me; you can't go wrong with a man like that. A great deal of the 'locations' in old Spanish California were in fact studio; I used powerful sun arcs to simulate sunlight, and once again the shadows cast were very hard. Those sun arcs started out as powerful as searchlights; when they came in they used to blind the cast – literally in one instance, a musical I worked on, in which the chorus girls were blinded: Klieg eyes, they called them.

Then came *Tobacco Road* for John Ford. And now you're talking about the director I liked working with better than anybody in the industry. You'd only talk, I think you might say, fifty words to him in a day; you had a communication with him so great you could *sense* what he wanted. He knew nothing of lighting; he never once looked in the camera when we worked together. You see, the man had bad eyes, as long as I knew him, but he was a man whose veins ran with the business. He had a tremendous memory; he could come up with an idea from some picture he had made thirty years before, and suggest you did that.

I've had people offer me money to give them the formula that Jack Ford used to direct. But he had no formula. He had one odd thing: he'd talk to someone way across the studio about a character to be played by someone sitting next to him, instead of talking to the man next to him about it, and the man next to him would of course listen to every word.

I'll give you an example of the way he worked. There was a scene in *How Green Was My Valley*: the girl was going to be married, and they were going to have this big party. There was

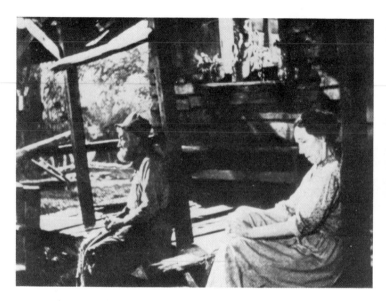

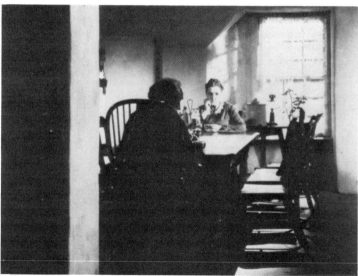

'Now you're talking about the director . . .': *Tobacco Road* and *How Green Was My Valley*

going to be all hell raised, beer and stuff, and he asked Donald Crisp, 'What do they do over in Scotland when they have such?' And Crisp said, 'They'd have a man see if he could hold his liquor; he'd draw a line with a piece of chalk and sing a song and walk on the line.' The art director figured the line would take up a big piece of the set, so Ford would just say to me, 'You know about how much of that you can get in?' And I said, 'Yes,' and he said, 'Where's the sideline?' And I'd say, 'That chair.' That's all the work he did; I'd do all the lighting, he'd never see through the lens, and in one take only we did the whole scene.

I always liked economy, and that's why I liked being with Jack; on that one we scarcely used a foot that wasn't in the final print (on a previous picture, *To Have and To Hold*, we shot half a million feet as against 100,000 on this one for the same length of story). Ford would make the best picture for less money than anyone I know. All the actors had to be punctual; nobody took a day off; he'd be improvising, changing freely all the time. But his eyesight was so bad he'd never compose; he'd leave everything to the cameraman.

I very much enjoyed making *The Song of Bernadette*. At the beginning of the picture, in Bernadette's home, when she first comes in, and stands there for a minute, you see a little glow on the wall, hardly noticeable, just like you would use to make the head stand away from an object behind it, but more intensified. I had this spotlight glow to the very end of the picture. And here is a perfect example of how little directors control things like this. When we looked at three cut reels Henry King said, 'Do you notice something?' And I said, 'What?' And he said, 'Every time she appears there's something glowing at the back of her head.' I don't know whether he thought this was something spiritual that had crept into the picture from heaven!

That was the good part of my time in pictures. You could do these things! You could add things for the picture on your own! Today the director tries to do everything. Incidentally, I photographed the niche for the Virgin Mary, and Fred Sersen of Special Effects put her in.

The Ox-Bow Incident was a very 'studio' picture. It went from sunset to sunrise. Rather hard if you tried to do it outside. The trouble is that if you shoot night for night you see only black in the distance; but in fact in the desert or plains at night you see objects vaguely out there; but they don't photograph. Similarly, in *Immortal Sergeant*, when Henry Fonda sees the mirage in the desert, all the effects just had to be done on the stage. And we tried to shoot some of the picture in the desert, but at 127 degrees we just came down with heat exhaustion. For the mirage I used steam in a tray; just put water in it and let the steam rise. I asked how they did the mirage effect in *Lawrence of Arabia*. And they didn't fake anything; they just used a long-focus lens, and they shot the heat rising between Lawrence and the man. Extraordinary.

The Keys of the Kingdom suffered very badly from artificiality. When the priest first comes into China it could just as well have been Balboa. *Anna and the King of Siam* had slightly more realism. We had an art director on the picture by the name of Richard Day . . . a wonderful artist, who painted in oils and pastels. Landscapes, everything. While we were preparing this picture, he took sick. He started to haemorrhage. We'd got him to hospital and found he had a tubercular kidney and had to be fattened up a little. Then the carpenters went on strike . . . it was strike year.

So Richard Day told them from the hospital bed to make the sets out of plaster. Not a speck of paint on them, nothing. About fourteen pieces, put together in different combinations. It turned out remarkably well. In the dinner scene, in which Rex Harrison is presiding as the King, I repeated the same effect I had done in the Maharani's dinner in *Rains Came*, with everything shining, and oil on everything. I lit Harrison from below, to emphasize the high cheekbones, just as I had done to give Gregory Peck a fine-drawn ascetic look in *The Keys of the Kingdom*. A soft key light, not a spot.

The Razor's Edge was directed by Edmund Goulding. I had known him since before he was an actor. When I went to England to do a picture in 1921 I had remembered him as a contact man to

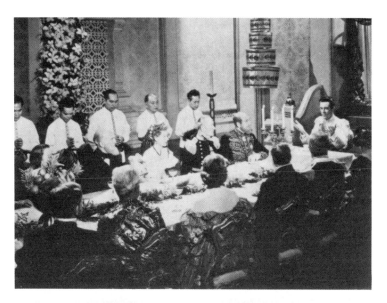

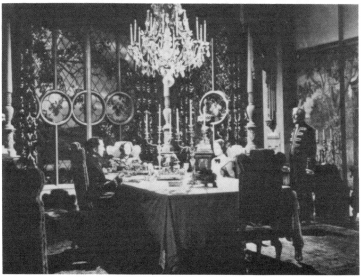

'Oiling the furniture': *Anna and the King of Siam* (Rex Harrison) and *Dragonwyck* (Vincent Price, Vivienne Osborne, Gene Tierney)

151

get us whatever we wanted. He knew everyone; I once photographed him with the Prince of Wales, who was a friend of his, at a garden-party. His idea of directing was to rehearse all morning and then shoot an entire scene in one take. Zanuck likes to *cut*. And to edit it all himself. After the first day's work, Zanuck said to me, 'Where are the close-ups?' And I said, 'The close-up is when the fellow turns around and looks up into the camera', and he said, 'Bullshit.' And I said, 'I told Goulding you wanted close-ups to work with in the cutting-room, but Goulding said, "I'm going to do it my way." ' So I told Zanuck to straighten it out. It wasn't too pleasant, and the fact is that Goulding really didn't know who looks left or who looks right in a cutting angle. If he did it all in one go he couldn't be wrong, he thought.

But it all became terribly pat; a man would take three steps and turn around and look into the camera . . . I'd call it 'One-two-three kick.' It made the picture mechanical. And I don't like long takes. Say what you will, the rhythm of a picture is in the cutting-room.

There was one bad lapse in the film. In the Himalayas there was a dreadful scene, with cardboard mountains. I almost died when I saw it. Zanuck said to me, 'What's wrong with it?' And I said, 'My God! It looks like something at Coney Island! It doesn't look real at all!' It was a fakey, phoney mess. But he wouldn't change it.

I liked working with Kazan on *Gentleman's Agreement*, but at that time he had no knowledge of technique either. He'd just give vague mechanical instructions. 'We'll follow her over here,' was about it, and I'd do the rest. It was a way-out Left picture, most of the cast were to the Left, Celeste Holm, Anne Revere, John Garfield, the whole damn lot, Jesus! We went up to Lake Mayopac in the Adirondacks for one scene; that's where all the Jewish people from New York go for their annual vacation. We stopped at a place on one side of the Lake that was like Washington slept there; the floors were bending and cracking. One night the assistant director and I went round the other side of the lake and there was another, nicer hotel, and we had dinner there. I went back and told Kazan we should switch hotels. He said we should go and

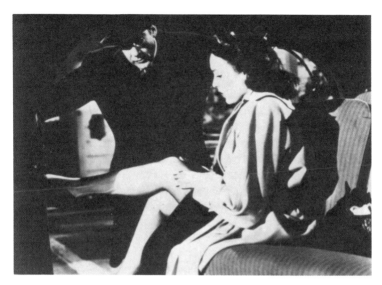

A Letter to Three Wives: Paul Douglas, Linda Darnell

make arrangements to transfer the company. And when I got there, the hotel manager looked at me and saw I was a gentile and said, 'I think you'd be happier with your own people on the other side of the lake!'

In *Letter to Three Wives* I again had a director who knew nothing about camera technique: Mankiewicz (I had worked on *Dragonwyck*). But *The Gunfighter* was a good deal more interesting: it was shot without any process at all, all that stuff with the guy waiting to shoot the man as he came out of a saloon from a high window . . . none of it was faked. The Western hats and clothes were exactly right.

I stripped *The Gunfighter* of all glamour. Henry King I always got on with; when we were making *Bernadette*, we had been doing three days in the girl's house when he said to me, 'Arthur, if I'd known we were going to shoot this picture from the floor I'd have worn my overalls!'

My very last picture was *The Prowler*, for Joseph Losey. I had trouble with Fox when Zanuck went to Europe, mainly contract problems; they refused to pay for my six-week vacation a year. They claimed they'd wired Zanuck and he'd supported the refusal; but I thought it was a lie. I said, 'All right, we'll just part friends.' And we did.

Just before that, I met Otto Preminger's brother at a party for the end of shooting of Preminger's *Whirlpool*, which I shot. And the brother asked me to make a film outside Fox, and I left them after eighteen and a half years . . . all, as I said, with the same unit.

So for Ingo Preminger I did *The Prowler*. Sam Spiegel was involved, too. He reminded me that I had done some work on *Tales of Manhattan*: a Sunday shot of a Negro minstrel band. And I remember meeting John Huston, who was also in this outfit, Horizon Pictures. Huston growled, 'Glad to have you aboard,' and all that crap . . . and we made a deal. Huston was supposed to direct *The Prowler*, but for some reason he couldn't. So Losey did it, in twenty-two days. It wasn't much. I was supposed to go on and do *The African Queen*, and I went to get the shots for various diseases. And through the examination the fellow found tuberculosis in my right lung. So I went home and went to bed for a year. I pulled out of it seventeen years ago, and the doctor said, 'Do you have to work?' I said 'No.' And he told me I'd live longer if I didn't work again. I went back to being an amateur photographer. Now I just do odds and ends here, and talk to fellows like you. I'm very happy.

Checklists

Leon Shamroy

Born New York, 16 July 1901. Educated at Cooper Union, New York, City College, New York, and Columbia University. Assistant to Nicholas J. Shamroy. Developed the Lawrence motor. Worked with Flaherty on *Acoma, The Sky City* (1928), the print of which was destroyed by fire. *Blindfold* (1928) was directed by Charles Klein, cameraman Lucien Andriot.

Feature films as Lighting Cameraman:

1927 *Tongues of Scandal* (d: Roy Clements); *Pirates of the Sky* (d: Charles Andrews); *The Trunk Mystery* (d: Frank H. Crane); *Catch-as-Catch-Can* (d: Charles Hutchinson); *Hidden Aces* (d: Howard Mitchell); *Land of the Lawless* (d: Tom Buckingham)

1928 *The Last Moment* (d: Paul Fejos); *Out with the Tide* (d: Charles Hutchinson); *Bitter Sweets* (d: Charles Hutchinson); [*The Tell-Tale Heart* (d: Charles F. Klein), a short film]

1930 *Alma de Gaucho* [in Spain] (U.S. title: *Soul of the Gaucho*. d: Henry Otto)

1931 *Women Men Marry* (d: Charles Hutchinson)

1932 *Stowaway* (d: Philip Whitman); *A Strange Adventure* (d: Philip Whitman, Hampton Del Ruth)

1933 *Jennie Gerhardt* (d: Marion Gering); *Her Bodyguard* (d: William Beaudine, co-ph: Harry Fishbeck); *Three-Cornered Moon* (d: Elliott Nugent)

1934 *Good Dame* (British title: *Good Girl*. d: Marion Gering); *Thirty Day Princess* (d: Marion Gering); *Kiss and Make-Up* (d: Harlan Thompson); *Ready for Love* (d: Marion Gering); *Behold My Wife!* (d: Mitchell Leisen)

1935 *Private Worlds* (d: Gregory La Cava); *She Married Her Boss* (d: Gregory La Cava); *Accent on Youth* (d: Wesley Ruggles); *She Couldn't Take It* (d: Tay Garnett); *Mary Burns, Fugitive* (d: William K. Howard)

1936 *Soak the Rich* (d: Ben Hecht, Charles MacArthur); *Fatal Lady* (d: Edward Ludwig); *Spendthrift* (d: Raoul Walsh); *Wedding Present* (d: Richard Wallace)

1937 *You Only Live Once* (d: Fritz Lang); *Her Husband Lies* (d: Edward Ludwig); *The Great Gambini* (d: Charles Vidor); *She Asked for It* (d: Erle C. Kenton); *Blossoms on Broadway* (d: Richard Wallace)

1938 *The Young in Heart* (d: Richard Wallace)

1939 *Made for Each Other* (d: John Cromwell); *The Story of Alexander Graham Bell* (British title: *The Modern Miracle*. d: Irving Cummings); *The Adventures of Sherlock Holmes* (British title: *Sherlock Holmes*. d: Alfred Werker)

1940 *Little Old New York* (d: Henry King); *I Was an Adventuress* (d: Gregory Ratoff, co-ph: Edward Cronjager); *Lillian Russell* (d: Irving Cummings); *Four Sons* (d: Archie Mayo); *Down Argentine Way* (d: Irving Cummings, co-ph: Ray Rennahan. Technicolor); *Tin Pan Alley* (d: Walter Lang)

1941 *That Night in Rio* (d: Irving Cummings, co-ph: Ray Rennahan. Technicolor); *The Great American Broadcast* (d: Archie Mayo, co-ph: Peverell Marley); *Moon Over Miami* (d: Walter Lang, co-ph: Peverell Marley, Allen M. Davey. Technicolor); *A Yank in the RAF* (d: Henry King); *Confirm or Deny* (d: Archie Mayo)

1942 *Roxie Hart* (d: William A. Wellman); *Ten Gentlemen from West Point* (d: Henry Hathaway); *The Black Swan* (d: Henry King. Technicolor)

1943 *Crash Dive* (d: Archie Mayo. Technicolor); *Stormy Weather* (d: Andrew Stone); *Claudia* (d: Edmund Goulding)

1944 *Buffalo Bill* (d: William A. Wellman. Technicolor); *Greenwich Village* (d: Walter Lang, co-ph: Harry Jackson. Technicolor); *Wilson* (d: Henry King. Technicolor)

1945 *A Tree Grows in Brooklyn* (d: Elia Kazan); *Where Do We Go From Here?* (d: Gregory Ratoff. Technicolor); *State Fair* (d: Walter Lang. Technicolor); *The Shocking Miss Pilgrim* (d: George Seaton)

1946 *Leave Her to Heaven* (d: John M. Stahl. Technicolor)

1947 *Forever Amber* (d: Otto Preminger. Technicolor); *Daisy Kenyon* (d: Otto Preminger)

1948 *That Lady in Ermine* (d: Ernst Lubitsch. Technicolor)

1949 *Prince of Foxes* (d: Henry King); *Twelve O'Clock High* (d: Henry King)

1950 *Cheaper by the Dozen* (d: Walter Lang. Technicolor); *Two Flags West* (d: Robert Wise)

1951 *On the Riviera* (d: Walter Lang. Technicolor); *David and Bathsheba* (d: Henry King. Technicolor)

1952 *With a Song in My Heart* (d: Walter Lang. Technicolor); *Wait Till the Sun Shines, Nellie* (d: Henry King. Technicolor); *Down Among the Sheltering Palms* (d: Edmund Goulding. Technicolor); *The Snows of Kilimanjaro* (d: Henry King. Technicolor)

1953 *Tonight We Sing* (d: Mitchell Leisen. Technicolor); *Call Me Madam* (d: Walter Lang. Technicolor); *The Girl Next Door* (d: Richard Sale. Technicolor); *White Witch Doctor* (d: Henry Hathaway. Technicolor); *The Robe* (d: Henry Koster. Technicolor, CinemaScope); *King of the Khyber Rifles* (d: Henry King. Technicolor, CinemaScope)

1954 *The Egyptian* (d: Michael Curtiz. DeLuxe Colour, CinemaScope); *There's No Business Like Show Business* (d: Walter Lang. DeLuxe Colour, CinemaScope)

1955 *Daddy Long Legs* (d: Jean Negulesco. DeLuxe Colour, CinemaScope); *Love Is a Many-Splendored Thing* (d: Henry King. DeLuxe Colour, CinemaScope); *Good Morning, Miss Dove* (d: Henry Koster. DeLuxe Colour, CinemaScope)

1956 *The King and I* (d: Walter Lang. DeLuxe Colour, CinemaScope 55); *The Best Things in Life Are Free* (d: Michael Curtiz. DeLuxe Colour, CinemaScope); *The Girl Can't Help It* (d: Frank Tashlin. DeLuxe Colour, CinemaScope)

1957 *The Desk Set* (British title: *His Other Woman*. d: Walter Lang. DeLuxe Colour, CinemaScope)

1958 *South Pacific* (d: Joshua Logan. Technicolor, Todd-AO); *The Bravados* (d: Henry King. DeLuxe Colour, CinemaScope); *Rally 'round the Flag, Boys!* (d: Leo McCarey. DeLuxe Colour, CinemaScope)

1959 *Porgy and Bess* (d: Otto Preminger. Technicolor, Todd-AO); *The Blue Angel* (d: Edward Dmytryk. DeLuxe Colour, CinemaScope); *Beloved Infidel* (d: Henry King. DeLuxe Colour, CinemaScope)

1960 *Wake Me When It's Over* (d: Mervyn LeRoy. DeLuxe Colour, Cinema-Scope); *North to Alaska* (d: Henry Hathaway. DeLuxe Colour, Cinema-Scope)

1961 *Snow White and the Three Stooges* (British title: *Snow White and the Three Clowns*. d: Walter Lang. DeLuxe Colour, CinemaScope)

1962 *Tender is the Night* [in France] (d: Henry King. DeLuxe Colour, Cinema-Scope)

1963 *Cleopatra* [in Italy] (d: Joseph L. Mankiewicz. DeLuxe Colour, Todd-AO); *The Cardinal* (d: Otto Preminger. Technicolor, Panavision)

1964 *What a Way to Go!* (d: J. Lee Thompson. DeLuxe Colour, CinemaScope); *John Goldfarb, Please Come Home* (d: J. Lee Thompson. DeLuxe Colour, CinemaScope)

1965 *The Agony and the Ecstasy* [in Italy] (d: Carol Reed. DeLuxe Colour, Todd-AO); *Do Not Disturb* (d: Ralph Levy. DeLuxe Colour, Cinema-Scope)

1966 *The Glass Bottom Boat* (d: Frank Tashlin. Metrocolor, Panavision)

1967 *Caprice* (d: Frank Tashlin. DeLuxe Colour, CinemaScope)

1968 *Planet of the Apes* (d: Franklin Schaffner. DeLuxe Colour, Panavision);
       The Secret Life of an American Wife (d: George Axelrod. DeLuxe
       Colour); *Skidoo* (d: Otto Preminger. Technicolor, Panavision)

1969 *Justine* (d: George Cukor. DeLuxe Colour, Panavision)

Lee Garmes

Born Peoria, Illinois, 1898. Educated at North Denver High School. Entered
films September 1916 in New York as an assistant cameraman; later moved to
Hollywood, where he worked for Thomas H. Ince. Between 1916 and 1924
worked as assistant on various comedy series including the Chester Comedies,
the Model Comedies, the Snooky Comedies, the Carter De Haven Comedies,
and twelve of the *Fighting Blood* films directed by Malcolm St Clair and Henry
Lehrman, and on *The Hope Chest* (1918) and *I'll Get Him Yet* (1919), both
produced by D. W. Griffith, who also supervised the direction.

Feature films as Lighting Cameraman:

1924 *Find Your Man* (d: Malcolm St Clair)

1925 *Keep Smiling* (d: Albert Austin, Gilbert Pratt); *The Goat Getter* (d: Albert
       S. Rogell)

1926 *The Grand Duchess and the Waiter* (d: Malcolm St Clair); *A Social
       Celebrity* (d: Malcolm St Clair); *The Palm Beach Girl* (d: Erle C.
       Kenton); *The Show Off* (d: Malcolm St Clair); *The Popular Sin* (d:
       Malcolm St Clair)

1927 *The Garden of Allah* (d: Rex Ingram); *Rose of the Golden West* (d: George
       Fitzmaurice); *The Private Life of Helen of Troy* (d: Alexander Korda);
       The Love Mart (d: George Fitzmaurice)

1928 *The Little Shepherd of Kingdom Come* (d: Alfred Santell); *The Yellow Lily*
       (d: Alexander Korda); *Waterfront* (d: William A. Seiter); *The Barker*
       (d: George Fitzmaurice)

1929 *His Captive Woman* (d: George Fitzmaurice); *Love and the Devil* (d:
       Alexander Korda); *Prisoners* (d: William A. Seiter); *Say It with Songs*
       (d: Lloyd Bacon); *Disraeli* (d: Alfred E. Green); *The Great Divide* (d:
       Reginald Barker)

1930 *Lilies of the Field* (d: Alexander Korda); *Song of the West* (d: Ray Enright);
       The Other Tomorrow (d: Lloyd Bacon); *Whoopee* (d: Thornton Free-
       land); *Morocco* (d: Josef von Sternberg); *Bright Lights* (d: Michael
       Curtiz)

1931 *Dishonoured* (d: Josef von Sternberg); *Fighting Caravans* (d: Otto Brower, David Burton); *City Streets* (d: Rouben Mamoulian); *Kiss Me Again* (British title: *Toast of the Legion*. d: William A. Seiter); *An American Tragedy* (d: Josef von Sternberg); *Confessions of a Co-ed* (British title: *Her Dilemma*. d: Dudley Murphy, David Burton)

1932 *Shanghai Express* (d: Josef von Sternberg); *Scarface* (d: Howard Hawks); *Strange Interlude* (British title: *Strange Interval*. d: Robert Z. Leonard); *Smilin' Through* (d: Sidney Franklin); *Call Her Savage* (d: John Francis Dillon)

1933 *Face in the Sky* (d: Harry Lachman); *Zoo in Budapest* (d: Rowland V. Lee); *Shanghai Madness* (d: John Blystone); *My Lips Betray* (d: John Blystone); *I Am Suzanne* (d: Rowland V. Lee)

1934 *George White's Scandals* (d: Thornton Freeland, Harry Lachman); *Crime Without Passion* (d: Ben Hecht, Charles MacArthur)

1935 *Once in a Blue Moon* (d: Ben Hecht, Charles MacArthur); *The Scoundrel* (d: Ben Hecht, Charles MacArthur)

1937 *Dreaming Lips* [in G.B.] (d: Paul Czinner. Garmes is credited as co-producer and technical supervisor)

1939 [*Gone with the Wind*] (d: Victor Fleming, co-ph: Ernest Haller, Ray Rennahan. Technicolor)

1940 *Angels over Broadway* (d: Ben Hecht, Lee Garmes)

1941 *Lydia* (d: Julien Duvivier)

1942 *Rudyard Kipling's Jungle Book* (British title: *The Jungle Book*. d: Zoltan Korda. Technicolor); *Footlight Serenade* (d: Gregory Ratoff); *China Girl* (d: Henry Hathaway)

1943 *Forever and a Day* (d: René Clair, Edmund Goulding, Cedric Hardwicke, Frank Lloyd, Victor Saville, Robert Stevenson, Herbert Wilcox, co-ph: Robert De Grasse, Russell Metty, Nicholas Musuraca); *Flight for Freedom* (d: Lothar Mendes)

1944 *Since You Went Away* (d: John Cromwell, co-ph: Stanley Cortez); *Guest In The House* (d: John Brahm); *None Shall Escape* (d: André De Toth)

1945 *Love Letters* (d: William Dieterle); *Paris Underground* (British title: *Madame Pimpernel*. d: Gregory Ratoff)

1946 *The Searching Wind* (d: William Dieterle); *Specter of the Rose* (British title: *Spectre of the Rose*. d: Ben Hecht); *Young Widow* (d: Edwin L. Marin); *Duel in the Sun* (d: King Vidor, co-ph: Hal Rosson, Ray Rennahan. Technicolor)

1947 *The Secret Life of Walter Mitty* (d: Norman Z. McLeod. Technicolor); *Nightmare Alley* (d: Edmund Goulding); *The Paradine Case* (d: Alfred Hitchcock)

1948 *Caught* (d: Max Ophuls)

1949 *My Foolish Heart* (d: Mark Robson); *The Fighting Kentuckian* (d: George Waggner); *Roseanna McCoy* (d: Irving Reis)

1950 *My Friend Irma Goes West* (d: Hal Walker); *Our Very Own* (d: David Miller)

1951 *Saturday's Hero* (British title: *Idols in the Dust*. d: David Miller); *That's My Boy* (d: Hal Walker); *Detective Story* (d: William Wyler); *Thunder in the East* (d: Charles Vidor)

1952 *The Captive City* (d: Robert Wise); *Actors and Sin* (d: Ben Hecht); *The Lusty Men* (d: Nicholas Ray)

1954 *Abdulla the Great* [in G.B. and Egypt] (U.S. title: *Abdullah's Harem*. d: Gregory Ratoff. Technicolor)

1955 *Land of the Pharaohs* (d: Howard Hawks, co-ph: Russell Harlan. Warner-Color, CinemaScope); *The Desperate Hours* (d: William Wyler. Vista-Vision); *Man with the Gun* (British title: *The Trouble Shooter*. d: Richard Wilson); *The Bottom of the Bottle* (British title: *Beyond the River*. d: Henry Hathaway. Eastman Colour, CinemaScope)

1956 *D-Day the Sixth of June* (d: Henry Koster. Eastman Colour, Cinema-Scope); *The Sharkfighters* (d: Jerry Hopper. Technicolor, Cinema-Scope); *The Big Boodle* (British title: *Night in Havana*. d: Richard Wilson)

1958 *Never Love a Stranger* (d: Robert Stevens)

1959 *The Big Fisherman* (d: Frank Borzage. Technicolor, Panavision); *Happy Anniversary* (d: David Miller)

1961 *Misty* (d: James B. Clark, co-ph: Leo Tover. DeLuxe Colour, Cinema-Scope)

1962 *Hemingway's Adventures of a Young Man* (d: Martin Ritt. DeLuxe Colour, CinemaScope)

1964 *Lady in a Cage* (d: Walter Grauman)

1966 *A Big Hand for the Little Lady* (British title: *Big Deal at Dodge City*. d: Fielder Cook. Technicolor)

1968 *How to Save a Marriage ... and Ruin Your Life* (d: Fielder Cook. Technicolor, Panavision)

Feature films as Director:

1937 *The Sky's the Limit* [in G.B.] (co-d: Jack Buchanan)

1940 *Angels over Broadway* (co-d: Ben Hecht)

Feature films as Associate Director:

1934 *Crime without Passion* (d: Ben Hecht, Charles MacArthur)

1935 *Once in a Blue Moon* (d: Ben Hecht, Charles MacArthur); *The Scoundrel* (d: Ben Hecht, Charles MacArthur)

1952 *Actors and Sin* (d: Ben Hecht)

Feature films as Producer:

1937 *The Lilac Domino* [in G.B.] (d: Frederick Zelmick)

1940 *Beyond Tomorrow* (d: A. Edward Sutherland)

1941 *Lydia* (d: Julien Duvivier)

Feature film as Associate Producer:

1946 *Specter of the Rose* (d: Ben Hecht)

William Daniels

Born Cleveland, Ohio, 1895. Educated at the University of Southern California. Assistant operator at Triangle (1917), then first operator at Universal (1918). Worked for Samuel Goldwyn (1922–3), and after a short period as a freelance in 1924 joined M–G–M where he worked until 1943, then he joined Universal.

Feature films as Lighting Cameraman:

1919 *Blind Husbands* (d: Erich von Stroheim)

1920 *The Devil's Passkey* (d: Erich von Stroheim)

1922 *Foolish Wives* (d: Erich von Stroheim, co-ph: Ben Reynolds); *The Long Chance* (d: Jack Conway)

1923 *Merry-Go-Round* (d: begun by Erich von Stroheim, completed by Rupert Julian, co-ph: Ben Reynolds)

1924 *Helen's Babies* (d: William A. Seiter)

1925 *Woman and Gold* (d: James P. Hogan); *Greed* (d: Erich von Stroheim, co-ph: Ben Reynolds); *The Merry Widow* (d: Erich von Stroheim, co-ph: Ben Reynolds)

1926 *Dance Madness* (d: Robert Z. Leonard); *Ibanez' Torrent* (d: Monta Bell); *Monte Carlo* (d: Christy Cabanne); *The Boob* (British title: *The Yokel*. d: William Wellman); *Money Talks* (d: Archie Mayo); *Bardelys the Magnificent* (d: King Vidor); *Altars of Desire* (d: Christy Cabanne)

1927 *The Flesh and the Devil* (d: Clarence Brown); *Captain Salvation* (d: John S. Robertson); *Tillie, the Toiler* (d: Hobart Henley)

1928 *Love* (British title: *Anna Karenina*. d: Edmund Goulding); *The Latest from Paris* (d: Sam Wood); *Bringing Up Father* (d: Jack Conway); *The Actress* (British title: *Trelawney of the Wells*. d: Sidney Franklin); *Telling the World* (d: Sam Wood); *The Mysterious Lady* (d: Fred Niblo); *Dream of Love* (d: Fred Niblo, co-ph: Oliver Marsh); *Woman of Affairs* (d: Clarence Brown)

1929 *A Lady of Chance* (d: Robert Z. Leonard, co-ph: Peverell Marley); *Wild Orchids* (d: Sidney Franklin); *The Trial of Mary Dugan* (d: Bayard Veiller); *The Last of Mrs Cheyney* (d: Sidney Franklin); *Wise Girls* (d: E. Mason Hopper); *The Kiss* (d: Jacques Feyder)

1930 *Their Own Desire* (d: E. Mason Hopper); *Anna Christie* (d: Clarence Brown. Also German version, d: Jacques Feyder); *Montana Moon* (d: Malcolm St Clair); *Strictly Unconventional* (d: David Burton, co-ph: Oliver Marsh); *Romance* (d: Clarence Brown)

1931 *The Great Meadow* (d: Charles Brabin, co-ph: Clyde De Vinna); *Inspiration* (d: Clarence Brown); *Strangers May Kiss* (d: George Fitzmaurice); *A Free Soul* (d: Clarence Brown); *Si l'Empereur Savait Ca* (d: Jacques Feyder; French version of *His Glorious Night* (1929), director Lionel Barrymore, ph: Percy Hilburn); *Susan Lenox, Her Fall and Rise* (British title: *The Rise of Helga.* d: Robert Z. Leonard)

1932 *Mata Hari* (d: George Fitzmaurice); *Lovers Courageous* (d: Robert Z. Leonard); *Grand Hotel* (d: Edmund Goulding); *As You Desire Me* (d: George Fitzmaurice); *Skyscraper Souls* (d: Edgar Selwyn)

1933 *Rasputin and the Empress* (British title: *Rasputin, the Mad Monk.* d: Richard Boleslawski); *The White Sister* (d: Victor Fleming); *The Stranger's Return* (d: King Vidor); *Broadway to Hollywood* (British title: *Ring Up the Curtain.* d: Willard Mack, co-ph: Norbert Brodine); *Dinner at Eight* (d: George Cukor); *Christopher Bean* (d: Sam Wood)

1934 *Queen Christina* (d: Rouben Mamoulian); *Barretts of Wimpole Street* (d: Sidney Franklin); *The Painted Veil* (d: Richard Boleslawski)

1935 *Naughty Marietta* (d: W. S. Van Dyke); *Anna Karenina* (d: Clarence Brown); *Rendezvous* (d: William K. Howard)

1936 *Rose-Marie* (d: W. S. Van Dyke); *Romeo and Juliet* (d: George Cukor); *Camille* (d: George Cukor, uncredited co-ph: Karl Freund)

1937 *Personal Property* (d: W. S. Van Dyke); *Broadway Melody of 1938* (d: Roy Del Ruth); *Double Wedding* (d: Richard Thorpe); *The Last Gangster* (d: Edward Ludwig); *Beg, Borrow, or Steal* (d: William Thiele)

1938 *Marie Antoinette* (d: W. S. Van Dyke); *Three Loves Has Nancy* (d: Richard Thorpe); *Dramatic School* (d: Robert B. Sinclair)

1939 *Idiot's Delight* (d: Clarence Brown); *Stronger Than Desire* (d: Leslie Fenton); *Ninotchka* (d: Ernst Lubitsch); *Another Thin Man* (d: W. S. Van Dyke, co-ph: Oliver Marsh)

1940 *The Shop Around the Corner* (d: Ernst Lubitsch); *The Mortal Storm* (d: Frank Borzage); *New Moon* (d: Robert Z. Leonard)

1941 *So Ends Our Night* (d: John Cromwell); *Back Street* (d: Robert Stevenson); *They Met in Bombay* (d: Clarence Brown); *Shadow of the Thin Man* (d: W. S. Van Dyke); *Design for Scandal* (d: Norman Taurog, co-ph: Leonard Smith); *Dr Kildare's Victory* (d: W. S. Van Dyke)

1942 *Keeper of the Flame* (d: George Cukor)

1943 *Girl Crazy* (d: Norman Taurog, co-ph: Robert Planck)

1947 *Brute Force* (d: Jules Dassin); *Lured* (British title: *Personal Column*. d: Douglas Sirk)

1948 *The Naked City* (d: Jules Dassin); *For the Love of Mary* (d: Frederick de Cordova); *Family Honeymoon* (d: Claude Binyon)

1949 *The Life of Riley* (d: Irving Brecher); *Illegal Entry* (d: Frederick de Cordova); *Abandoned* (d: Joe Newman); *The Gal Who Took the West* (d: Frederick de Cordova. Technicolor); *Woman in Hiding* (d: Michael Gordon)

1950 *Winchester '73* (d: Anthony Mann); *Harvey* (d: Henry Koster); *Deported* (d: Robert Siodmak)

1951 *Thunder on the Hill* (British title: *Bonaventure*. d: Douglas Sirk); *Bright Victory* (British title: *Lights Out*. d: Mark Robson); *The Lady Pays Off* (d: Douglas Sirk)

1952 *When in Rome* [in Italy] (d: Clarence Brown); *Pat and Mike* (d: George Cukor); *Glory Alley* (d: Raoul Walsh); *Plymouth Adventure* (d: Clarence Brown. Technicolor)

1953 *Never Wave at a WAC* (British title: *The Private Wore Skirts*. d: Norman Z. McLeod); *Forbidden* (d: Rudolph Maté); *Thunder Bay* (d: Anthony Mann. Technicolor); *The Glenn Miller Story* (d: Anthony Mann. Technicolor)

1954 *War Arrow* (d: George Sherman. Technicolor); *The Far Country* (d: Anthony Mann. Technicolor)

1955 *Six Bridges to Cross* (d: Joseph Pevney); *Foxfire* (d: Joseph Pevney. Technicolor); *The Shrike* (d: José Ferrer); *Strategic Air Command* (d: Anthony Mann. Technicolor, VistaVision); *The Girl Rush* (d: Robert Pirosh. Technicolor, VistaVision); *The Benny Goodman Story* (d: Valentine Davies. Technicolor)

1956 *Away All Boats!* (d: Joseph Pevney, co-ph: Clifford Stine. Technicolor, VistaVision); *The Unguarded Moment* (d: Harry Keller. Technicolor); *Istanbul* (d: Joseph Pevney. Technicolor, CinemaScope)

1957 *Night Passage* (d: James Neilson. Technicolor, Technirama); *Interlude* [in Germany and Austria] (d: Douglas Sirk. Technicolor, CinemaScope); *My Man Godfrey* (d: Henry Koster. Eastman Colour, CinemaScope)

1958 *Voice in the Mirror* (d: Harry Keller. CinemaScope); *Cat on a Hot Tin Roof* (d: Richard Brooks. Metrocolor); *Some Came Running* (d: Vincente Minnelli. Metrocolor, CinemaScope); *A Stranger in My Arms* (d: Helmut Käutner. CinemaScope)

1959 *A Hole in the Head* (d: Frank Capra. DeLuxe Colour, CinemaScope); *Never So Few* (d: John Sturges. Metrocolor, CinemaScope)

1960 *Can-Can* (d: Walter Lang. Technicolor, Todd-AO); *All the Fine Young Cannibals* (d: Michael Anderson. Metrocolor, CinemaScope); *Ocean's 11* (d: Lewis Milestone. Technicolor, Panavision)

1961 *Come September* [in Italy] (d: Robert Mulligan. Technicolor, Cinema-Scope)

1962 *How the West Was Won* (d: John Ford, Henry Hathaway, George Marshall, co-ph: Milton Krasner, Charles Lang, jun., Joseph LaShelle. Technicolor, Cinerama); *Billy Rose's Jumbo* (d: Charles Walters. Metrocolor, Panavision)

1963 *Come Blow Your Horn* (d: Bud Yorkin. Technicolor, Panavision); *The Prize* (d: Mark Robson. Metrocolor, Panavision)

1964 *Robin and the 7 Hoods* (d: Gordon Douglas. Technicolor, Panavision)

1965 *Von Ryan's Express* [in Italy] (d: Mark Robson. DeLuxe Colour, Cinema-Scope); *Marriage on the Rocks* (d: Jack Donohue. Technicolor, Panavision)

1966 *Assault on a Queen* (d: Jack Donohue. Technicolor, Panavision)

1967 *In Like Flint* (d: Gordon Douglas. DeLuxe Colour, CinemaScope); *Valley of the Dolls* (d: Mark Robson. DeLuxe Colour, Panavision)

1968 *The Impossible Years* (d: Michael Gordon. Metrocolor, Panavision); *Marlowe* (d: Paul Bogart. Metrocolor)

1969 *The Maltese Bippy* (d: Norman Panama. Metrocolor, Panavision)

Feature films as Producer:

1965 *Marriage on the Rocks* (d: Jack Donohue)

1966 *Assault on a Queen* (d: Jack Donohue)

James Wong Howe

Born Kwantung, China, 1899 (real name: Wong Tung Jim); from 1904: U.S.A. At first a professional boxer. From 1917 to 1922 assistant to Alvin Wyckoff (Cecil B. De Mille's photographer), then camera operator. Known simply as James Howe until 1933, when M–G–M publicized him as a Chinese camera-man.

Feature films as Lighting Cameraman:

1922 *Drums of Fate* (British title: *Drums of Destiny*. d: Charles Maigne)

1923 *The Trail of the Lonesome Pine* (d: Charles Maigne); *The Woman with Four Faces* (d: Herbert Brenon); *To the Last Man* (d: Victor Fleming); *The Spanish Dancer* (d: Herbert Brenon)

1924 *The Breaking Point* (d: Herbert Brenon); *The Side Show of Life* (d: Herbert Brenon); *The Alaskan* (d: Herbert Brenon); *Peter Pan* (d: Herbert Brenon)

1925 *The Call of the Canyon* (d: Victor Fleming); *The Charmer* (d: Sidney Olcott); *Not So Long Ago* (d: Sidney Olcott); *The Best People* (d: Sidney Olcott); *The King on Main Street* (d: Monta Bell. Sequences in Technicolor)

1926 *The Song and Dance Man* (d: Herbert Brenon); *Sea Horses* (d: Allan Dwan); *Mantrap* (d: Victor Fleming); *Padlocked* (d: Allan Dwan)

1927 *The Rough Riders* (d: Victor Fleming); *Sorrell and Son* [in G.B.] (d: Herbert Brenon)

1928 *Laugh, Clown, Laugh* (d: Herbert Brenon); *The Perfect Crime* (d: Bert Glennon); *Four Walls* (d: William Nigh)

1929 *Desert Nights* (d: William Nigh)

1930 *Today* (d: William Nigh)

1931 *Transatlantic* (d: William K. Howard); *The Criminal Code* (d: Howard Hawks); *The Spider* (d: William Cameron Menzies, Kenneth McKenna); *The Yellow Ticket* (British title: *The Yellow Passport*. d: Raoul Walsh); *Surrender* (d: William K. Howard)

1932 *Dance Team* (d: Sidney Lanfield); *After Tomorrow* (d: Frank Borzage); *Amateur Daddy* (d: John Blystone); *Man about Town* (d: John Francis Dillon); *Chandu the Magician* (d: William Cameron Menzies, Marcel Varnel)

1933 *Walking Down Broadway* (d: Erich von Stroheim. Not released. Re-edited and partly re-shot as *Hello Sister* with no director credited); *Hello Sister* (see *Walking Down Broadway*); *The Power and the Glory* (d: William K. Howard); *Beauty for Sale* (d: Richard Boleslawski); *Viva Villa!* (d. Jack Conway, co-ph: Charles G. Clarke)

1934 *The Show-Off* (d: Charles F. Reisner); *The Thin Man* (d: W. S. Van Dyke); *Manhattan Melodrama* (d: W. S. Van Dyke); *Hollywood Party* (d: Richard Boleslawski. Sequence in Technicolor); *Stamboul Quest* (d: Sam Wood); *Have a Heart* (d: David Butler); *Biography of a Bachelor Girl* (d: Edward H. Griffith)

1935 *The Night is Young* (d: Dudley Murphy); *Mark of the Vampire* (d: Tod Browning); *The Flame Within* (d: Edmund Goulding); *O'Shaughnessy's Boy* (d: Richard Boleslawski); *Three Live Ghosts* (d: H. Bruce Humberstone, co-ph: Chester Lyons)

1936 *Whipsaw* (d: Sam Wood); *Fire Over England* [in G.B.] (d: William K. Howard); *Farewell Again* [in G.B.] (Originally titled *Troopship*. d: Tim Whelan, co-ph: Hans Schneeberger); *Under the Red Robe* [in G.B.] (d: Victor Sjöström, co-ph: Georges Périnal)

1937 *The Prisoner of Zenda* (d: John Cromwell); *The Adventures of Tom Sawyer* (d: Norman Taurog. Technicolor)

1938 *Algiers* (d: John Cromwell); *Comet Over Broadway* (d: Busby Berkeley)

1939 *They Made Me a Criminal* (d: Busby Berkeley); *The Oklahoma Kid* (d: Lloyd Bacon); *Daughters Courageous* (d: Michael Curtiz); *Dust Be My Destiny* (d: Lewis Seiler); *On Your Toes* (d: Ray Enright); *Abe Lincoln in Illinois* (British title: *Spirit of the People*. d: John Cromwell)

1940 *The Story of Dr Ehrlich's Magic Bullet* (d: William Dieterle); *Saturday's Children* (d: Vincent Sherman); *Torrid Zone* (d: William Keighley); *City for Conquest* (d: Anatole Litvak, co-ph: Sol Polito); *A Dispatch from Reuters* (British title: *This Man Reuter*. d: William Dieterle); *The Strawberry Blonde* (d: Raoul Walsh)

1941 *Shining Victory* (d: Irving Rapper); *Out of the Fog* (d: Anatole Litvak); *Kings Row* (d: Sam Wood)

1942 *Yankee Doodle Dandy* (d: Michael Curtiz); *The Hard Way* (d: Vincent Sherman); *Hangmen Also Die* (d: Fritz Lang. Reissued in 1950 as *Lest We Forget*)

1943 *Air Force* (d: Howard Hawks); *The North Star* (British title: *North Star*. d: Lewis Milestone. Reissued in America as *Armored Attack*)

1944 *Passage to Marseille* (d: Michael Curtiz)

1945 *Objective Burma!* (d: Raoul Walsh); *Counter Attack* (British title: *One Against Seven*. d: Zoltan Korda); *Confidential Agent* (d: Herman Shumlin); *Danger Signal* (d: Robert Florey); *My Reputation* (d: Curtis Bernhardt)

1947 *Nora Prentiss* (d: Vincent Sherman); *Pursued* (d: Raoul Walsh); *Body and Soul* (d: Robert Rossen)

1948 *Mr Blandings Builds His Dream House* (d: H. C. Potter); *The Time of Your Life* (d: H. C. Potter)

1949 *The Eagle and the Hawk* (d: Lewis R. Foster. Technicolor)

1950 *The Baron of Arizona* (d: Samuel Fuller); *Tripoli* (d: William Price. Technicolor)

1951 *The Brave Bulls* (d: Robert Rossen); *He Ran All the Way* (d: John Berry); *Behave Yourself* (d: George Beck); *The Lady Says No* (d: Frank Ross)

1953 *Main Street to Broadway* (d: Tay Garnett); *Come Back, Little Sheba* (d: Daniel Mann)

1955 *The Rose Tattoo* (d: Daniel Mann. VistaVision); *Picnic* (d: Joshua Logan)

1956 *Death of a Scoundrel* (d: Charles Martin); *Drango* (d: Hall Bartlett, Jules Bricken)

1957 *The Sweet Smell of Success* (d: Alexander Mackendrick); *The Old Man and the Sea* (d: John Sturges. WarnerColor, add. ph: Floyd Crosby, Tom Tutweiler)

1958 *Bell, Book and Candle* (d: Richard Quine. Technicolor)

1959 *The Last Angry Man* (d: Daniel Mann); *The Story on Page One* (d: Clifford Odets)

1960 *Song Without End* (d: Charles Vidor, George Cukor. Eastman Colour, CinemaScope); *Tess of the Storm Country* (d: Paul Guilfoyle. DeLuxe Colour, CinemaScope)

1962 *Hud* (d: Martin Ritt. Panavision)

1964 *The Outrage* (d: Martin Ritt. Panavision)

1965 *The Glory Guys* (d: Arnold Laven. DeLuxe Colour, Panavision)

1966 *Seconds* (d: John Frankenheimer); *This Property Is Condemned* (d: Sydney Pollack. Technicolor)

1967 *Hombre* (d: Martin Ritt. DeLuxe Colour, Panavision)

1968 *The Heart Is a Lonely Hunter* (d: Robert Ellis Miller. Technicolor)

1969 *The Molly Maguires* (d: Martin Ritt. Technicolor, Panavision); *Blood Kin* (d: Sidney Lumet)

Feature films as Director:

1954 *Go, Man, Go* (ph: Bill Steiner)

1957 *The Invisible Avenger* (co-d: John Sledge, ph: Willis Winford, Joseph Wheeler)

Short film as Director:

1953 *The World of Dong Kingman* (also ph.)

In 1930 Wong Howe produced, directed and photographed a Japanese film (title unknown) which was shown in Japan, and in 1948 he began work in China on the background for a film to be called *Rickshaw Boy*, but the project was abandoned. He has also worked in television in America.

Stanley Cortez

Born (Stanley Krantz) New York, 4 November 1908. Educated at New York University. Worked with several portrait photographers (Steichen, Pirie MacDonald, Bachrach, etc.). Assistant cameraman from 1926, and later second cameraman for various studios.

Feature films as Lighting Cameraman:

1936 *Four Days' Wonder* (d: Sidney Salkow)

1937 *The Wildcatter* (d: Lewis D. Collins); *Armored Car* (d: Lewis R. Foster)

1938 *The Black Doll* (d: Otis Garrett); *Lady in the Morgue* (British title: *The Case of the Missing Blonde*. d: Otis Garrett); *Danger on the Air* (d: Otis Garrett); *Personal Secretary* (d: Otis Garrett); *The Last Express* (d: Otis Garrett)

167

1939 *Risky Business* (d: Arthur Lubin); *For Love or Money* (British title: *Tomorrow at Midnight.* d: Albert S. Rogell); *They Asked For It* (d: Frank McDonald); *The Forgotten Woman* (d: Harold Young); *Hawaiian Nights* (d: Albert S. Rogell); *Laugh It Off* (British title: *Lady Be Gay.* d: Albert S. Rogell)

1940 *Alias the Deacon* (d: Christy Cabanne); *Love, Honor, and Oh, Baby!* (d: Charles Lamont); *The Leatherpushers* (d: John Rawlins); *Margie* (d: Otis Garrett, Paul Gerard Smith); *Meet the Wildcat* (d: Arthur Lubin); *A Dangerous Game* (d: John Rawlins)

1941 *The Black Cat* (d: Albert S. Rogell); *San Antonio Rose* (d: Charles Lamont); *Moonlight in Hawaii* (d: Charles Lamont); *Badlands of Dakota* (d: Alfred E. Green); *Bombay Clipper* (d: John Rawlins)

1942 *The Magnificent Ambersons* (d: Orson Welles); *Eagle Squadron* (d: Arthur Lubin)

1943 *The Powers Girl* (British title: *Hello Beautiful.* d: Norman Z. McLeod); *Flesh and Fantasy* (d: Julien Duvivier, co-ph: Paul Ivano)

1944 *Since You Went Away* (d: John Cromwell, co-ph: Lee Garmes)

1947 *Smash-Up* (British title: *A Woman Destroyed.* d: Stuart Heisler)

1948 *Secret Beyond the Door* (d: Fritz Lang); *Smart Woman* (d: Edward A. Blatt)

1949 *The Man On the Eiffel Tower* (d: Burgess Meredith. Ansco Colour)

1950 *The Underworld Story* (Originally released in U.S. as *The Whipped.* d: Cyril Endfield); *The Admiral Was a Lady* (d: Albert S. Rogell)

1951 *The Basketball Fix* (British title: *The Big Decision.* d: Felix Feist); *Fort Defiance* (d: John Rawlins. Cinecolor)

1952 *Models, Inc.* (Released in G.B. as *Call Girl*, re-released in G.B. as *That Kind of Girl.* d: Reginald LeBorg); *Abbott and Costello Meet Captain Kidd* (d: Charles Lamont. Supercinecolor)

1953 *The Diamond Queen* (d: John Brahm. Supercinecolor); *Dragon's Gold* (d: Aubrey Wisberg, Jack Pollexfen); *Shark River* (d: John Rawlins. Vivid Color by the Color Corporation of America)

1954 *Riders to the Stars* (d: Richard Carlson. Color Corporation of America); *Black Tuesday* (d: Hugo Fregonese)

1955 *The Night of the Hunter* (d: Charles Laughton)

1956 *Man From Del Rio* (d: Harry Horner)

1957 *Top Secret Affair* (British title: *Their Secret Affair.* d: H. C. Potter); *The Three Faces of Eve* (d: Nunnally Johnson. CinemaScope)

1959 *Thunder in the Sun* (d: Russell Rouse. Technicolor); *Vice Raid* (d: Edward L. Cahn); *The Angry Red Planet* (d: Ib Melchior. Eastman Colour)

1960 *Dinosaurus!* (d: Irwin S. Yeaworth, jun. DeLuxe Colour, CinemaScope)

1961 *Back Street* (d: David Miller. Eastman Colour)

1963 *Shock Corridor* (d: Samuel Fuller); *Nightmare in the Sun* (d: Marc Lawrence. DeLuxe Colour)

1964 *The Naked Kiss* (d: Samuel Fuller)

1966 *Ghost in the Invisible Bikini* (d: Don Weis. Pathécolor, Panavision)

1968 *Blue* (d: Silvio Narizzano. Technicolor, Panavision)

1969 *The Bridge at Remagen* [in Europe] (d: John Guillermin. DeLuxe Colour, Panavision)

Short film as Director:

1932 *Scherzo* (also ph. and sc.)

Karl Struss

Born New York, 1891. Took courses in art photography at Columbia University, and in 1914 set up his own photographic studio specializing in publicity and magazine photographs. Joined Cecil B. De Mille in 1919. Worked for B. P. Schulberg for three years, and from 1927–1930 with D. W. Griffith. Joined Paramount in 1931.

Feature films as Lighting Cameraman:

1920 *Something to Think About* (d: Cecil B. De Mille)

1921 *The Affairs of Anatol* (d: Cecil B. De Mille); *The Law and the Woman* (d: Penryhn Stanlaws); *Fool's Paradise* (d: Cecil B. De Mille)

1922 *Saturday Night* (d: Cecil B. De Mille); *Fools First* (d: Marshall Neilan); *Rich Men's Wives* (d: Louis Gasnier); *Thorns and Orange Blossoms* (d: Louis Gasnier); *Minnie* (d: Marshall Neilan, Frank Urson); *The Hero* (d: Louis Gasnier)

1923 *Poor Men's Wives* (d: Louis Gasnier); *Daughters of the Rich* (d: Louis Gasnier); *Mothers-in-Law* (d: Louis Gasnier); *Maytime* (d: Louis Gasnier)

1924 *White Man* (d: Louis Gasnier); *Poisoned Paradise* (d: Louis Gasnier); *The Legend of Hollywood* (d: Renaud Hoffman); *Idle Tongues* (d: Lambert Hillyer)

1925 *The Winding Stair* (d: John Griffith Wray. Tinted sequences)

1926 *Hell's 400* (British title: *Just and Unjust*. d: John Griffith Wray. Tinted); *Sparrows* (British title: *Human Sparrows*. d: William Beaudine, co-ph: Charles Rosher); *Meet the Prince* (d: Joseph Henabery); *Forever After* (d: F. H. Weight)

1927 *Sunrise* (d: F. W. Murnau, co-ph: Charles Rosher); *Ben Hur* (d: Fred Niblo, in collaboration with twelve other cameramen)

1928 *Drums of Love* (d: D. W. Griffith, co-ph: Harry Jackson, Billy Bitzer); *The Night Watch* (d: Alexander Korda); *Battle of the Sexes* (d: D. W. Griffith, co-ph: Billy Bitzer)

1929 *Lady of the Pavements* (d: D. W. Griffith, co-ph: Billy Bitzer); *Coquette* (d: Sam Taylor); *The Taming of the Shrew* (d: Sam Taylor)

1930 *Lummox* (d: Herbert Brenon); *Be Yourself* (d: Thornton Freeland, co-ph: Robert Planck); *One Romantic Night* (d: Paul L. Stein); *The Bad One* (d: George Fitzmaurice); *Abraham Lincoln* (d: D. W. Griffith); *Danger Lights* (d: George Seitz, co-ph: John Boyle)

1931 *Kiki* (d: Sam Taylor); *Skippy* (d: Norman Taurog); *Up Pops the Devil* (d: A. Edward Sutherland); *Women Love Once* (d: Edward Goodman); *Murder by the Clock* (d: Edward Sloman); *The Road to Reno* (d: Richard Wallace)

1932 *Dr Jekyll and Mr Hyde* (d: Rouben Mamoulian); *Two Kinds of Women* (d: William C. De Mille); *Dancers in the Dark* (d: David Burton); *The World and the Flesh* (d: John Cromwell); *Forgotten Commandments* (d: Louis Gasnier, William Schorr. With episodes from De Mille's *The Ten Commandments*); *The Man from Yesterday* (d: Berthold Viertel); *Guilty as Hell* (British title: *Guilty as Charged.* d: Erle C. Kenton); *The Sign of the Cross* (d: Cecil B. De Mille); *Island of Lost Souls* (d: Erle C. Kenton)

1933 *Tonight Is Ours* (d: Stuart Walker); *The Woman Accused* (d: Paul Sloane); *The Story of Temple Drake* (d: Stephen Roberts); *The Girl in 419* (d: Alexander Hall, George Somnes); *Disgraced* (d: Erle C. Kenton); *Torch Singer* (d: Alexander Hall, George Somnes)

1934 *Four Frightened People* (d: Cecil B. De Mille); *Belle of the Nineties* (d: Leo McCarey); *The Pursuit of Happiness* (d: Alexander Hall); *Here is My Heart* (d: Frank Tuttle)

1935 *Goin' to Town* (d: Alexander Hall); *Two for Tonight* (d: Frank Tuttle)

1936 *Anything Goes* (alternative title: *Tops is the Limit.* d: Lewis Milestone); *The Preview Murder Mystery* (d: Robert Florey); *Too Many Parents* (d: Robert F. McGowan); *Rhythm on the Range* (d: Norman Taurog); *Hollywood Boulevard* (d: Robert Florey); *Go West, Young Man* (d: Henry Hathaway); *Let's Make a Million* (d: Raymond McCarey)

1937 *Waikiki Wedding* (d: Frank Tuttle); *Mountain Music* (d: Robert Florey); *Double or Nothing* (d: Theodore Reed); *Thunder Trail* (d: Charles Barton)

1938 *Every Day's a Holiday* (d: A. Edward Sutherland); *Thanks for the Memory* (d: George Archainbaud); *Sing, You Sinners* (d: Wesley Ruggles)

1939 *Paris Honeymoon* (d: Frank Tuttle); *Zenobia* (d: Gordon Douglas); *Some Like It Hot* (d: George Archainbaud); *Island of Lost Men* (d: Kurt Neumann); *The Star Maker* (d: Roy Del Ruth)

1940 *The Great Dictator* (d: Charlie Chaplin, co-ph: Roland Totheroh)

1941 *Caught in the Draft* (d: David Butler); *Aloma of the South Seas* (d: Alfred Santell. Technicolor)

1943 *Happy Go Lucky* (d: Curtis Bernhardt, co-ph: Wilfred Cline, Ellsworth Hoagland); *Journey into Fear* (d: Norman Foster); *Riding High* (British title: *Melody Inn*. d: George Marshall, co-ph: Harry Hallenberger. Technicolor)

1944 *And the Angels Sing* (d: George Marshall); *Rainbow Island* (d: Ralph Murphy. Technicolor)

1945 *Bring on the Girls* (d: Sidney Lanfield. Technicolor); *Tarzan and the Leopard Woman* (d: Kurt Neumann)

1946 *Suspense* (d. Frank Tuttle); *Mr Ace* (d: Edwin L. Marin)

1947 *The Macomber Affair* (d: Zoltan Korda, co-ph: O. H. Borradaile, John Wilcox, Freddie Francis); *Heaven Only Knows* (d: Albert S. Rogell)

1948 *The Dude Goes West* (d: Kurt Neumann); *Siren of Atlantis* (d: Arthur Ripley, Gregg G. Tallas); *Tarzan's Magic Fountain* (d: Lee Sholem)

1949 *Bad Boy* (d: Kurt Neumann)

1950 *Rocketship XM* (d: Kurt Neumann. Part in colour); *It's a Small World* (d: William Castle); *The Return of Jesse James* (d: Arthur David Hilton); *The Texan Meets Calamity Jane* (d: Ande Lamb. Cinecolor); *Father's Wild Game* (d: Herbert I. Leeds)

1951 *Tarzan's Peril* (British title: *Tarzan and the Jungle Queen*. d: Byron Haskin)

1952 *Rose of Cimarron* (d: Harry Keller. Natural Colour); *Tarzan's Savage Fury* (d: Cyril Endfield); *Limelight* (d: Charlie Chaplin)

1953 *Tarzan and the She-Devil* (d: Kurt Neumann); *Il Piu Comico Spettacolo del Mondo* [in Italy] (d: Mario Mattoli, co-ph: Fernando Riri, Riccardo Pallottini. Ferraniacolor, 3-D); *Il Turco Napoletano* [in Italy] (d: Mario Mattoli, co-ph: Riccardo Pallottini. Ferraniacolor, 3-D); *Cavalleria Rusticana* [in Italy] (U.S. title: *Fatal Desire*. d: Carmine Gallone, co-ph: Riccardo Pallottini. Ferraniacolor)

1954 *Attila* [in Italy] (alternative Italian title: *Attila, Flagello di Dio*. British title: *Attila the Hun*. d: Pietro Francisci, co-ph: Aldo Tonti, Luciano Trasatti. Technicolor); *Due Notte con Cleopatra* [in Italy] (d: Mario Mattoli, co-ph: Riccardo Pallottini. Ferraniacolor)

1955 *Mohawk* (d: Kurt Neumann. Eastman Colour, Widevision)

1957 *She Devil* (d: Kurt Neumann. RegalScope); *Kronos* (d: Kurt Neumann. RegalScope); *The Deerslayer* (d: Kurt Neumann. DeLuxe Colour, CinemaScope)

1958 *The Rawhide Trail* (d: Robert Gordon); *The Fly* (d: Kurt Neumann. DeLuxe Colour, CinemaScope); *The Hot Angel* (d: Joe Parker); *Machete* (d: Kurt Neumann)

1959 *The Sad Horse* (d: James B. Clark. DeLuxe Colour, CinemaScope); *Here Come the Jets* (d: Gene Fowler, jun. RegalScope); *The Rebel Set* (d: Gene Fowler, jun.)

Arthur Miller

Born July 8, 1895, Roslyn, Long Island

Feature films as Lighting Cameraman:

1918 *A Japanese Nightingale* (d: George Fitzmaurice); *The Narrow Path* (d: George Fitzmaurice)

1919 *Common Clay* (d: George Fitzmaurice); *The Cry of the Weak* (d: George Fitzmaurice); *The Profiteers* (d: George Fitzmaurice); *Our Better Selves* (d: George Fitzmaurice); *A Society Exile* (d: George Fitzmaurice); *Counterfeit* (d: George Fitzmaurice)

1920 *On With the Dance* (d: George Fitzmaurice); *His House in Order* (d: Hugh Ford); *Lady Rose's Daughter* (d: Hugh Ford); *The Right to Love* (d: George Fitzmaurice); *Idols of Clay* (d: George Fitzmaurice)

1921 *Paying the Piper* (d: George Fitzmaurice); *Experience* (d: George Fitzmaurice)

1922 *Forever* (British title: *Peter Ibbetson*. d: George Fitzmaurice); *To Have and to Hold* (d: George Fitzmaurice); *Kick In* (d: George Fitzmaurice)

1923 *Bella Donna* (d: George Fitzmaurice); *The Cheat* (d: George Fitzmaurice); *The Eternal City* (d: George Fitzmaurice)

1924 *Cytherea* (British title: *Forbidden Way*. d: George Fitzmaurice); *Tarnish* (d: George Fitzmaurice); *In Hollywood with Potash and Perlmutter* (d: Al Green); *A Thief in Paradise* (d: George Fitzmaurice)

1925 *His Supreme Moment* (d: George Fitzmaurice); *The Coming of Amos* (d: Paul Sloane); *Made for Love* (d: Paul Sloane)

1926 *The Volga Boatman* (d: Cecil B. De Mille); *Eve's Leaves* (d: Paul Sloane); *The Clinging Vine* (d: Paul Sloane); *For Alimony Only* (d: William De Mille)

1927 *Nobody's Widow* (d: Donald Crisp); *Vanity* (d: Donald Crisp); *The Fighting Eagle* (British title: *The Brigadier Gerard*. d: Donald Crisp); *The Angel of Broadway* (d: Lois Weber)

1928 *The Blue Danube* (d: Paul Sloane); *Hold 'em Yale* (d: Edward H. Griffith); *The Cop* (d: Donald Crisp); *Annapolis* (d: Christy Cabanne); *The Spieler* (d: Tay Garnett); *Bellamy Trial* (British title: *The Bellamy Trial*. d: Monta Bell)

1929 *Strange Cargo* (d: Arthur Gregor, silent version; Benjamin Glazer, sound version); *The Flying Fool* (d: Tay Garnett); *Sailor's Holiday* (d: Fred Newmeyer); *Big News* (d: Gregory La Cava); *Oh, Yeah!* (British title: *No Brakes*. d: Tay Garnett)

1930 *Officer O'Brien* (d: Tay Garnett); *Behind the Make-Up* (d: Monta Bell); *His First Command* (d: Gregory La Cava, co-ph: J. J. Mescall; *The Lady of Scandal* (British title: *The High Road*. d: Sidney Franklin, co-ph: Oliver Marsh); *The Truth About Youth* (d: William A. Seiter); *See America Thirst* (d: William James Craft, co-ph: Allyn Jones)

1931 *Father's Son* (d: William Beaudine); *Bad Company* (d: Tay Garnett); *The Big Shot* (British title: *The Optimist*. d: Ralph Murphy)

1932 *Panama Flo* (d: Ralph Murphy); *Young Bride* (d: William A. Seiter); *Okay America* (British title: *The Penalty of Fame*. d: Tay Garnett); *Breach of Promise* (d: Paul L. Stein); *Me and My Gal* (British title: *Pier 13*. d: Raoul Walsh)

1933 *Sailor's Luck* (d: Raoul Walsh); *Hold Me Tight* (d: David Butler); *The Man Who Dared* (d: Hamilton McFadden); *The Last Trail* (d: James Tinling); *My Weakness* (d: David Butler); *The Mad Game* (d: Irving Cummings)

1934 *Ever Since Eve* (d: George Marshall); *Bottoms Up* (d: David Butler); *Handy Andy* (d: David Butler); *Love Time* (British title: *Lovetime*. d: James Tinling); *The White Parade* (d: Irving Cummings); *Bright Eyes* (d: David Butler)

1935 *The Little Colonel* (d: David Butler); *It's a Small World* (d: Irving Cummings); *Black Sheep* (d: Allan Dwan); *Welcome Home* (d: James Tinling)

1936 *Paddy O'Day* (d: Lewis Seiler); *White Fang* (d: David Butler); *36 Hours to Kill* (d: Eugene Ford); *Pigskin Parade* (British title: *The Harmony Parade*. d: David Butler); *Stowaway* (d: William A. Seiter)

1937 *Wee Willie Winkie* (d: John Ford); *Heidi* (d: Allan Dwan)

1938 *The Baroness and the Butler* (d: Walter Lang); *Rebecca of Sunnybrook Farm* (d: Allan Dwan); *Little Miss Broadway* (d: Irving Cummings); *Submarine Patrol* (d: John Ford)

1939 *The Little Princess* (d: Walter Lang, co-ph: William Skall); *Susannah of the Mounties* (d: William A. Seiter); *The Rains Came* (d: Clarence Brown); *Here I Am a Stranger* (d: Roy Del Ruth)

1940 *The Blue Bird* (d: Walter Lang. Technicolor); *Johnny Apollo* (d: Henry Hathaway); *On Their Own* (d: Otto Brower); *The Mark of Zorro* (d: Rouben Mamoulian)

1941 *Tobacco Road* (d: John Ford); *Man Hunt* (d: Fritz Lang); *The Men in Her Life* (d: Gregory Ratoff); *How Green Was My Valley* (d: John Ford)

1942 *This Above All* (d: Anatole Litvak); *Iceland* (British title: *Katina*. d: Bruce Humberstone); *The Ox-Bow Incident* (British title: *Strange Incident*. d: William A. Wellman); *Immortal Sergeant* (d: John M. Stahl, co-ph: Clyde De Vinna)

1943 *The Moon Is Down* (d: Irving Pichel); *The Song of Bernadette* (d: Henry King)

1944 *The Purple Heart* (d: Lewis Milestone); *The Keys of the Kingdom* (d: John M. Stahl)

1945 *A Royal Scandal* (British title: *Czarina*. d: Otto Preminger)

1946 *Dragonwyck* (d: Joseph L. Mankiewicz); *Anna and the King of Siam* (d: John Cromwell); *The Razor's Edge* (d: Edmund Goulding)

1947 *Gentleman's Agreement* (d: Elia Kazan)

1948 *The Walls of Jericho* (d: John M. Stahl)

1949 *A Letter to Three Wives* (d: Joseph L. Mankiewicz)

1950 *Whirlpool* (d: Otto Preminger); *The Gunfighter* (d: Henry King)

1951 *The Prowler* (d: Joseph Losey)

Acknowledgements

Checklists compiled by Jan Dawson

Stills by courtesy of 20th Century-Fox, M-G-M, United Artists, Paramount, Warner-Pathé, Universal, Disney, Gala and the Stills Library of the National Film Archive.

The author and editors are grateful to all the cameramen interviewed for making this book possible, and would also like to thank Stanley Cortez, Karl Struss and Mr. and Mrs. Wong Howe for their generous loan of stills and portraits.

Index

Titles in This Series

1.
Roy Armes. Patterns of Realism. 1971

2.
Iris Barry. D. W. Griffith: American Film Master: with an annotated list of films by Eileen Bowser. 1965
bound with
Richard Griffith. Samuel Goldwyn: The Producer and His Films. 1956

3.
Ingmar Bergman. Four Screenplays: Smiles of a Summer Night, The Seventh Seal, Wild Strawberries, The Magician. 1960

4.
Luis Bunuel. Three Screenplays: Viridiana, The Exterminating Angel, Simon of the Desert. 1969

5.
Jean Cocteau. Cocteau on the Film. 1954

6.
Bosley Crowther. The Lion's Share. 1957

7.
Cecil B. DeMille. The Autobiography of Cecil B. DeMille. 1959

8.
Denis Gifford. The British Film Catalogue, 1895–1970. 1973

9.
Abel Green and Joe Laurie, Jr. Show Biz from Vaude to Video. 1951

10.
Robert M. Henderson. D. W. Griffith: His Life and Work. 1972

11.
Charles Higham. Hollywood Cameramen. 1970

12.
Ian C. Jarvie. Movies and Society. 1970

13.
John Howard Lawson. Film in the Battle of Ideas. 1953

14.
John Howard Lawson. Theory and Technique of Playwriting and Screenwriting. Revised edition. 1949

15.
Michael F. Mayer. Foreign Films on American Screens. 1965

16.
Vladimir Nilsen. The Cinema as a Graphic Art. 1959

17.
Robert Richardson. Literature and Film. 1969

18.
Donald Richie. George Stevens: An American Romantic. 1970

19.
Lillian Ross. Picture. 1952

20.
Roberto Rossellini. The War Trilogy: Open City, Paisan, Germany—Year Zero. 1973

21.
Robert Rossen. Three Screenplays: All the King's Men, The Hustler, Lilith. 1972

22.
Mack Sennett. King of Comedy. 1954

23.
Albert E. Smith, with Phil A. Koury. Two Reels and a Crank. 1952

24.
Bob Thomas. Selznick. 1970

25.
Bob Thomas. Thalberg: Life and Legend. 1969

26.
Parker Tyler. Chaplin: Last of the Clowns. 1948

27.
Parker Tyler. The Hollywood Hallucination. 1944

28.
Parker Tyler. Magic and Myth of the Movies. 1947

29.
Luchino Visconti. Two Screenplays: La Terra Trema, Senso. 1970

30.
Luchino Visconti. Three Screenplays: White Nights, Rocco and His Brothers, The Job. 1970

DATE DUE

AUG 1 9 1988			